Python for Beginners: Learn Python Programming With No Coding Experience in 7 Days

The Easiest & Quickest Way to Learn Python Coding, Programming, Web-Programming. Be a Python Programmer

By Santos Ozoemena

Table of Contents

Introduction 6

Chapter 1: Back to the Beginning 12
- Windows 18
- MacOS 18
- Linux 19
- **Installing Jupyter Notebook** 19

Chapter 2: Basic Python Syntax 22
- New Line 26
- String Concatenation 27
- Indentation 28

Chapter 3: Variables 30
- What is a variable? 30
- Rules to name variables in Python 31
- Variable Assignments 32
- Deleting a variable 37
- Reserved Keywords 37

Chapter 4: Operators for Variables 40
- Arithmetic Operators 41
  - Addition Operator + 41
  - Subtraction Operator 42
  - Multiplication Operator 42
  - Division Operator 42
  - Modulus Operator 43
  - Exponentiation or power operator 43
- Comparison Operator 46
  - "==" operator 46
  - ">" operator 47
  - "<" operator 47
  - ">=" operator 48
  - "<=" operator 48
  - "!=" operator 49
- Logical Operator 49
- Bitwise Operator 53

Chapter 5: Strings 59
What are strings? 59
How to use Strings? 60
Types of Strings 60
String Concatenation 61
Details of Strings 62
Check if a word is present in a string 63
Check if a word is not present in a string 64

Chapter 6: Tuples, List, and Dictionary 66
Tuple 67
List 69
Properties of Lists 69
Dictionary 70

Chapter 7: Statements and Loops 74

Chapter 8: Functions 80
8.1 Function vs Method 81
8.2 Defining a Function 81
8.3 Calling a Function 85
8.4 Returning Results from a Function 85
8.5 Returning Multiple Values from a Function 86

Chapter 9: Modules and Classes 89

Chapter 10: Opening and Closing Files 95

Chapter 11: Map, Filters, and Reduce 99
Map 99
Filters 100
Reduce 101

Data Structures and Algorithms 103
Arrays 103
Hash Tables 108
Stacks and Queues 109
Queue 109
Binary Search 110

Common Interview Questions 113

Multiple Choice Questions 120
Answers 124

Applications 126
Test Your Skills 130
Conclusion 139
Appendix 140

Introduction

“Programming isn’t about what you know; it’s about what you can figure out.” -by Chris Pine

Do you know what is considered the most sought-after skill in this decade? Analyzing big chunks of data and deriving insights from them is a skill that can help you change or transform your career. Learning to code does not have to be difficult anymore. Long gone are the days when you had to go to a university to get a computer science degree to learn how to code and write software. If you wish to learn how to code in a fun and enjoyable manner, then the book you are holding in your hands is the best book you could find on the market. In this book, you will learn the very basics of Programming and I will personally hold your hand as you progress through this book. We will begin the book by introducing the Python programming language. Python is considered to be one of the most popular programming languages, and anyone who is willing to put a bit of time and effort can learn to master this beautiful language. Once you have had the foundational knowledge of Python, we will begin by introducing the concept of variables, functions, loops, etc. Don’t worry if these concepts sound foreign to you right now. As you progress through the book, you will find all these esoteric concepts easy to grasp and within no time, you will be able to build your very own Python application. Most programming books start with the theory without giving any real-world examples and applications. In this book, we will explain all programming concepts by building a small calculator application. A calculator application is very easy to understand on the surface, but as you go along programming your own calculator app, you will learn the nuances of writing good code that others can use for their day-to-day activities.

A calculator application has all the components that you would need to understand the theory of computation and converting abstract concepts to code. You will be introduced to simple data structures like arrays, lists, dictionaries etc. You will then learn how to represent a number and store it in your computer’s memory. We will then build upon our skills to perform simple mathematical operations like addition, subtraction, multiplication, and division. If it has been some time since you have touched your Mathematics books, you don’t have to worry. We will start from the very basics, and you will see how these basic concepts relate to real-world applications. Once you get comfortable with these basic mathematical operations, we will shift our focus by introducing the concept of functions and classes. A function is used to avoid writing the same code again and again. Writing functions and avoiding duplication of code will be your stepping-stone to writing modular code - a skill even experienced developers haven't learned to master. In the last section of this book, you will get an introduction to object-oriented programming. Writing good code and structuring your code as your project gets bigger is a very important skill and could benefit you immensely. I have structured this book in small chunks which are easily digestible. You can start by reading one chapter every day. Here is how this book is structured:

Chapter 1: In Chapter 1 of this book, I will give you the motivation to learn Python as your first programming language. You will see some practical applications of Python. Once we know why we should learn Python, we can get all our tools ready. To start programming, we need an integrated development environment or a code editor. We will install VS Code and PyCharm. I will show you both the options to set up your development environment. If you are just getting started, I would recommend you go along by installing VS Code. Once we have our environment setup, we will code our very first "Hello World" program. You will learn how to execute a Python program from your terminal.

Chapter 2: In Chapter 2 you will learn the basic syntax of Python. You will be introduced to some best practices of writing good code. You will learn the ins and outs of the Python programming language. Furthermore, you will also learn how to comment your code and the motivation behind writing good comments.

Chapter 3: In Chapter 3 you will learn about variables and data-types. You will learn how to represent integers and floating-point numbers in Python. You will learn how to take two or more numbers and perform some common mathematical operations on them. Defining variables and performing operations on these variables are the nuts and bolts of any programming language.

Chapter 4: In Chapter 4 you will be introduced to the concept of mathematical operators. You will learn about some common operations like addition, subtraction, multiplication, division, and comparison.

Chapter 5: In Chapter 5 you will learn how to represent strings in Python. A string is a collection of characters and as a Python programmer, you would have to work with strings on a day-to-day basis. This chapter will set you on your path to perform common operations like calculating the length of a string or concatenating two strings, etc.

Chapter 6: In Chapter 6 you will learn about two important data structures to store your numbers. As you go from being a novice to a ninja programmer, having a thorough understanding of data structures will save you a lot of time and make you a more efficient and productive developer.

Chapter 7: In this chapter, you will learn about loops and control structures. You will use the concepts that you learned from the previous days to understand the concept of loops. Your assignment would be to implement a function to call another function multiple times.

Chapter 8: In this chapter, you will learn about functions and modular programming. A function is a piece of code that can be called multiple times. We will help you write functions by calculating the factorial of a number.

Chapter 9: In this chapter of the book you will be introduced to the concept of object-oriented programming, You will learn how to write maintainable code. We will implement a class called Calculator and will implement functions or methods to perform addition, subtraction, multiplication, and division. You will be introduced to concepts like encapsulation, inheritance, and composition. You don't have to worry about these concepts right now. Everything will become clear once you have the foundational knowledge of Programming and Python.

Chapter 10: In the chapter 10 of the book, you will learn about files and how to work with files in Python. File manipulation is an important concept and will be the stepping stone to read contents from files and process them for advanced applications like NLP, text processing, etc.

Chapter 11: In the final chapter of the book, you will be introduced to the concept of functional programming. We will look at lambda expressions and how to use filter, map and reduce functions in Python.

Who am I?

I spent years learning the craft of programming and getting better at it. I have been in your shoes and I wish I had a resource like the book you are reading now when I was getting started. My name is Santos and I have discovered the secret to learning programming effectively without wasting a lot of time. If you have read this far, that means you are really motivated to learn to program. Learning programming is a skill that can never go to waste. You will have a plethora of opportunities once you master this skill. You can use this skill to start building your own applications, working at a tech company, or dive deeper by learning about data science, machine learning, etc. The foundational knowledge of all these fields is programming and Python. Let me help you go from a novice to a ninja programmer. Let me tell you how I got started.

The year I got really hooked on python programming was my senior year in college back in 2017. I was introduced to programming by my late friend/brother named Felix. Felix was a software engineering major at my school, and I would always wonder what the hell is software engineering? What do you software engineers do exactly?. He would always tell me, but the information would enter one ear and leave the other. I was always so confused about exactly what he was talking about. At the time, I was majoring in Health Administration, which focuses on Healthcare, so unrelated to software engineering. I knew that Health administration was not the field I wanted to go into, but I majored in it anyway just to make mom and dad happy.

As I got closer to graduation, I was required to intern at a hospital to complete my course credit, which will allow me to graduate with a BS degree in Healthcare Administration. My role as an intern was to collect data, report on that data, create visualizations in a dashboard or excel and sometimes email my findings to directors or managers. This workflow sometimes took the whole day. This process became so tedious and boring. I just knew I can be doing so much more with my time than this. I kindly ask my manager, is there something else I can do besides this. She kindly told me this is all we have for you. She quickly rebutted and said if you can get that process done before your shift is over, I can put you on two other exciting projects. My manager, knowing this process took the whole shift, knew that it wouldn't happen. At that point, I felt stuck and couldn't wait till this boring internship was over.

I went home unsatisfied with my manager's response and thought to myself, There's got to be a way to get this done fast and efficiently, so I can free up my time to do other things. I went home and called my boy Felix and complained to him about what I was experiencing and what I can do to help. He quickly stated, 'seems like you need some automation done, have you considered looking into python ?' I responded with, 'what ?' He said 'python is one of the best programming languages used for automation, automating workflows and tasks.' At that moment, I felt like a light bulb lit up in my brain. He then recommended some courses to me. I took that course and many other courses. It took me about 6 months to get really comfortable with python programming. Once I got comfortable with python, it was then time for applying this knowledge to my internship.

So, there were three tasks I wanted to be automated:

1. Collecting data.
2. Reporting, Visualizations, and Dashboarding using Excel.
3. Email reports to managers or directors.

To automate data collection, I had to first understand where I was getting data from. I was collecting data from a database software used by many Hospitals to collect information about patients and health records. I would normally just log into this application like any other application and click what I wanted and download the data to my computer. I learned in Python that most applications have APIs (Application Programming Interface) or like a back door to get information from that application or database programmatically. I did my research and found the documentation of the API used for that application. I successfully set it up and was able to run my python script and pull the desired data I normally collect manually. This was my first win. I no longer needed to log in, navigate to the data I wanted and click download, I could just run my python script instead, and it would do all the work for me.

Automating reporting, visualization, and dashboarding was tricky but doable. In python, there is a library called Matplotlib which allows you to make custom bar charts, histograms, line charts just like what I was doing in Excel. So, instead of doing my reporting in Excel, I did it all in Matplotlib, then saved the result to an Excel document. This took some time, but remember you will only do it once. So, this task is done. What's left is emailing this result to my manager. At the time, the hospital I was interning at used outlook for their email domain. So, I quickly asked myself 'is there a way I can send emails without having to log into Outlook, click compose email, insert my report as an attachment and click send?' The answer is yes, I can. As you may know by now, python has many libraries and API integrations. I used a window's outlook library, which allowed me to do just that.

So, I created all the tasks in python, and what was left for me to do was to put all the tasks together and schedule them to run every morning at 9:30 am. I used a library call *scheduler* that allows you to schedule any python script. So, there you have it, my whole internship was replaced by the python code that I built. I arrived at work at 10:00 am one morning and my boss asked me, how did you get all the reporting done before your shift started? I said I used python to automate my whole workflow. She was so confused, but impressed. She later said, 'you damn millennials are so lazy. At that point, my manager had no projects for me to work on, and she stated 'You've just replaced 4 jobs and might have saved us a lot of money, you should be proud of yourself '. I felt bad about replacing jobs, but hey I just want to work smarter, not harder.

After this scenario, I feel it's important to understand or be familiar with the various python libraries that help advance my career and ultimately increase my salary as a Data Scientist.

A FREE GIFT TO OUR READERS

7 surprising beginner mistakes you should avoid as a beginner programmer downloadable guideline. This will set you on the right path to learning how to program.

santosbooks.com

Chapter 1: Back to the Beginning

What is Python?

If you are just getting started with programming, then you have made the right choice by learning Python. Python is one of the most popular languages and can be used for web development, building graphical user interfaces, analyzing data, and building machine learning applications. Python is a dynamically typed language, which makes it easy to learn and build applications in no time. Python has a huge ecosystem of open source libraries and a supportive community which makes it easy to get started.

Python is used in some of these fields:

1. Data Science

Data Science is the science of doing exploratory data analysis and finding patterns and trends in your data. You can use classical statistical algorithms or more sophisticated machine learning and deep learning algorithms for anomaly detection, time-series prediction, image classification, language translation, etc.

2. Web development

You can use Python for web development to build fast and reliable backend applications. You can use Python to connect to a database to fetch data from it and render it to the user in a front-end application. You can implement many basic web development features like authentication, fetching data, transforming data, securing data, and rendering them.

3. Software Engineering

Python can be used to develop software applications in many industries like Finance, Automotive, Retail, etc. A good deal of popular software as a service applications runs on Python. Python is also used to develop applications that run on edge devices like Raspberry-Pi and Nvidia Jetson. You can develop IoT applications to connect to sensors and develop applications like weather forecasting systems, humidity and temperature controller, Fintech applications like payment gateways, E -commerce shops, etc.

4. Game Development

Python is also used to develop games. There are many python bindings that connect to popular graphic libraries implemented in C or C++. Developing games in Python makes the implementation process easy and quick.

5. Automation

Python is also used to develop Robotics and automation applications. You can build prototype applications like self-driving cars, robotics applications that control an appliance based on sensor values. Many large industrial plants have robots deployed, with the core logic to control these robots implemented in Python.

Why should you learn Python?

1. Easy to learn

Python, unlike C++, is an interpreted language rather than a compiled one. You can get started without setting up a complex development environment. You don't have to worry about defining types for variables and objects, making it very flexible to start learning Programming with Python.

2. Versatile

Python is one of the few programming languages that can be used in various tasks. If you are interested in becoming a web developer, popular frameworks like Django, Flask, and FastAPI use Python. If you are someone who is more interested in Machine Learning or Artificial Intelligence, Python is the best language to learn because of a huge ecosystem of supporting packages and libraries like TensorFlow, PyTorch, and sci-kit-learn. Not only is its popularity tied to its convenience in learning, but Python is also very versatile and user-friendly. You can use Python in various things such as data science, data analysis, and even software engineering. Other programmers have used Python for statistical computing, data visualization, web development, machine learning, deep learning, artificial intelligence, web scraping, data engineering, game and mobile app development, and process automation. The fact that Python can be used in various fields of work and careers, makes it one of the most common programming languages.

3. Huge demand

According to a recent report published by Stack Overflow, Python is considered to be the most wanted language and the 3rd most loved language in the developer community. There is a lot of demand for good Python developers in different industries like Finance, Healthcare, Retail. With Python on your C.V., you would have a plethora of job opportunities.

4. Creative

Programming is not just about being logical. What differentiates an average programmer from a good is one's creativity. Learning Python and developing large-scale applications will help you unleash your creativity and contribute to your team's success.

5. Large Library

In the last couple of years, there has been a surge in the number of libraries developed in Python. There is a Python library for any imaginable task. With Python in your toolkit, you shall never have to reinvent the wheel from scratch. You can start building and deploying applications related to computer vision, speech processing, search, etc. within days.

6. Resources

Most beginners feel intimidated by programming due to the lack of support and overabundance of information. There is a friendly and supportive community that can help you if you are ever stuck. Popular websites like Stack Overflow and Stack Exchange will never make you feel alone.

7. Big data, Machine Learning and Cloud Computing

Cloud computing, Machine Learning, and Big Data are some of the hottest trends in the computer science world right now, which helps lots of organizations to transform and improve their processes and workflows. Python language is the second most popular used tool after R language for data science and analytics. A lot of many data processing workloads in the organization are powered by python language only. Most of the research and development takes place in python language due to its many applications, including ease of analyzing and organizing the usable data. Not only this but hundreds of python libraries are being used in thousands of machine learning projects every day, such as TensorFlow for neural networks and OpenCV for computer vision, etc.

According to The U.S. Bureau of Labor Statistics (BLS) anticipates data-related occupations will grow by 12 percent by 2028, creating over 546,200 new jobs in the same time period. Increasingly, top companies are in need of qualified professionals to fill those emerging roles. However, professionals with these specialized skills are difficult to find, which means data jobs pay quite well for those with the right expertise. This simply means there's so much room to learn and develop your skill set. Python is a very popular language used in data-related occupations, and you know what, It's not hard to learn. Below, I'll list the Top 10 Big Data careers.

1) Big Data Engineer
Annual Salary Range: $130,000-$222,000

Big data engineers are similar to data analysts in that they turn large volumes of data into insights that organizations can use to make smarter business decisions, but they're also tasked with retrieving, interpreting, analyzing, and reporting on a business's data—which they typically have to gather from a variety of different sources.

These professionals are also often responsible for creating and maintaining the company's software and hardware architecture, including the systems and processes users need to work with that data.

2) Data Architect
Annual Salary Range: $119,750-$193,500

These professionals are tasked with designing the structure of complex data frameworks, as well as building and maintaining these databases. Data architects develop strategies for each subject area of the enterprise data model and communicate plans, status, and issues to their company's executives.

3) Data Warehouse Manager
Annual Salary Range: $80,000-$160,250

Data warehouse managers are responsible for the storage and analysis of data in facilities. These professionals use performance and usage metrics to evaluate data, analyze data load, and monitor job usage. They may be responsible for identifying and mitigating potential risks to data storage and transfer.

4) Database Manager
Annual Salary Range: $111,250-$186,500

Database managers identify problems that occur in databases, take corrective action to remedy those issues, and assist with the design and physical implementation of storage hardware and maintenance.

These professionals work closely with database developers and often provide guidance and training to lower-level staff.

5) Business Intelligence Analyst
Annual Salary Range: $87,500-$185,500

Business intelligence analysts turn companies' data into insights that executives can use to make better business decisions. These professionals often respond to management's requests for specific information, but might also be expected to scrutinize data independently to find patterns and trends.

Business intelligence analysts should have a strong background in analytical and reporting tools, several years of experience with database queries and stored procedure writing, as well as online analytical processing (OLAP) and data cube technology skills.

6) Data Scientist
Annual Salary Range: $105,750-$180,250

Data scientists design and construct new processes for modeling, data mining, and production. In addition to conducting data studies and product experiments, these professionals are tasked with developing prototypes, algorithms, predictive models, and custom analysis.

Previous work experience in a similar position is usually required, and data scientists should be skilled in different data mining techniques, such as clustering, regression analysis, and decision trees.

7) Data Modeler
Annual Salary Range: $80,750-$170,000

These professionals turn large volumes of data into insights, such as micro and macro trends, which are gathered into reports for businesses. Data modelers must be skilled in both information science and statistical analysis, and should have proficient programming skills.

Data modelers often choose to specialize in a particular business area, which makes it easier to find useful data trends for their employers.

8) Database Developer
Annual Salary Range: $101,250-$172,750

Database developers are responsible for analyzing current database processes in order to modernize, streamline, or eliminate inefficient coding. These professionals are often charged with monitoring database performance, developing new databases, and troubleshooting issues as they arise.

Database developers work closely with other members of the development team. They're often required to have prior experience with database development, data analysis, and unit testing.

9) Database Administrator
Annual Salary Range: $79,250-$160,500

These professionals are responsible for monitoring and optimizing database performance to avoid damaging effects caused by constant access and high traffic. They also coordinate with IT security professionals to ensure data security. Database administrators typically have prior experience working on database administration teams.

10) Data Analyst
Annual Salary Range: $83,750-$142,500

Data analysts work with large volumes of data, turning them into insights businesses can leverage to make better decisions. They work across a variety of industries—from healthcare and finance to retail and technology.

Data analysts work to improve their own systems to make relaying future insights easier. The goal is to develop methods to analyze large data sets that can be easily reproduced and scaled.

Most of these roles might require you to have some level of experience or a graduate-level degree. However, you can always start as an analyst, which is entry-level. Once you have the python programming down and become very fluent, more doors and opportunities start to open up. There is more to becoming any of these professions as listed, but learning Python will give you the confidence you need to pursue more education and knowledge.

Installing the Python Program

Let us begin our journey to learning Python by installing Python on your computer. We will go through installing Python on Windows, Mac, and a Linux operating system.

Windows

In this section, we will learn how to install Python on a Windows machine.

In this section, we will look at the steps to install Python from the official Python downloader page.

1. Navigate to the official Downloads page for Windows. (https://www.python.org/downloads/windows/)
2. Under Stable Release, you will see the latest stable release. At the time of writing this book, the latest Python version available for download is 3.9.5.
3. Click on the Download Windows installer (64-bit).
4. Open the .exe file that was downloaded and follow the installation instructions.
5. You would have an option to change the installation path. The default path would be AppData/directory.
6. Click on Install now to finish the installation process.
7. Congratulations, you have successfully installed Python on your Windows machine.

MacOS

In this section, we will learn how to install Python on a Mac machine.

Downloading from the official page.

In this section, we will look at the steps to install Python from the official Python downloader page.

8. Navigate to the official Downloads page for MacOS.
   (https://www.python.org/downloads/macos/)
9. Under Stable Release, you will see the latest stable release. At the time of writing this book, the latest Python version available for download is 3.9.5.
10. Click on the Download macOS 64-bit Intel installer.
11. Open the pkg file that was downloaded and follow the instructions by pressing continue.
12. Once you click on Agree, you will be shown the location of the installation path.
13. Click on Close to close the installer.
14. Congratulations, you have successfully installed Python on your MacOS.

Linux

In this section, we will learn how to install Python on Ubuntu 18.04.

1. Open your terminal window.
2. Most Linux distributions come installed with Python. You can check the version of Python installed on your Linux distribution using python --version.
3. We will now install the latest version of Python on your computer. In the terminal window, execute the following commands
   a. sudo apt-get update
   b. sudo apt-get install python3.8 python3-pip
4. You can now type python3.8 in your terminal window and the interactive python shell will be activated.
5. Congratulations, you have successfully installed Python on your Linux machine.

Installing Jupyter Notebook

Jupyter notebook is a very popular tool for quick prototyping and learning Python. In this section, you will learn how to install Jupyter notebook on your computer and starting the notebook on your computer. Let us begin.

Navigate to your terminal window and install Jupyter notebook by executing the following command:

```
pip install notebook
```

Once Jupyter notebook is installed, you can execute the following command to start the notebook:

```
jupyter notebook
```

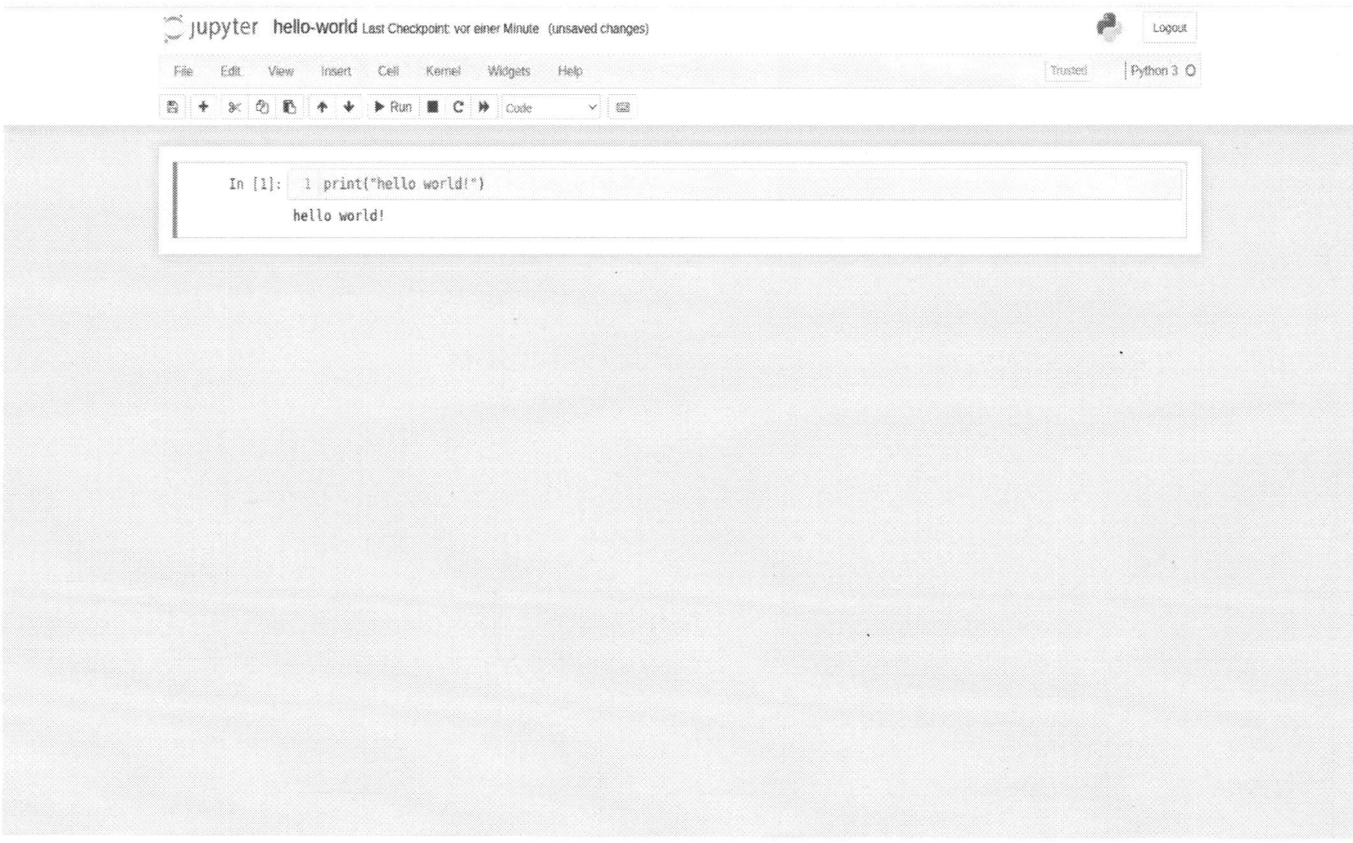

You can now start writing simple programs in the cell and executing them by pressing the Ctrl+ Enter or Shift+ Enter command on your keyboard.

Here's a full video on how to do this https://www.youtube.com/watch?v=aHdy0sXLGt0 **SKIP TO 2:46**. Very straight to the point.

NOTES

Chapter 2: Basic Python Syntax

What is a syntax?

Just like a human language follows rules of grammar, a programming language needs to follow some rules. A syntax defines a set of principles on how variables, functions, classes should be named. Let us take a simple example of defining a function in Python. In Chapter 8 you will learn more about functions. A function is identified by the def keyword. In the example below, you see a function called *add_sum* to return the sum of the two numbers. We observe that the function is prepended with the def keyword and the output of the function is returned by the return keyword. The # symbol indicates a single-line comment which describes the purpose of the function.

Python

```
def add_sum(a,b):
    # A function to add two numbers
    return a+b
```

Comments in Python

Programming is not just about writing code. Your code would have to be maintained and extended over the coming years. A good programmer also needs to learn how to document his code. Let us look at some ways to document and comment on our code in Python.

There are two ways to write a comment in Python - a single-line comment and a multi-line comment.

Single Line Comment

A single-line comment begins with a # symbol and should have no more than 80 characters.
Let us look at an example of writing a single-line comment:

```
Python

def greet(name):
    # A function to  greet someone
    return 'Hello' + name
```

In the above example, we have added a comment to describe the purpose of the function. As soon as the function greet() is called, you will see a string that greets you with the name that you pass to the function. The line with the comment is not executed since internally Python ignores lines with comments, and has no effect on the execution of the function.

Multi-Line Comment

A multi-line comment begins with triple quotes and ends with triple quotes. A multi -line comment is used to give information about the parameters and argument of a function, module, or a class.

```
Python

def mean(x):
    """
    Function to calculate the mean of a list of numbers
    ;param x: list of numbers
    ;return mean of the numbers
    """
    return sum(x)/(len(x))
```

Print Statement

As the first step to learning programming, it is important to know how to print or display information on your terminal windows. Python has an in -built function called print that helps us in printing a value on the screen. Let us see an example:

```
print("Hello World")
```

On executing the above command, you can see "Hello World" printed on the screen.

Triple, Double, and Single Quotes

In this section, we look at different ways of printing a string value.

You can use single, double, or triple quotes to print a string. For example, let us say we would like to print **Learning Python is fun.** We can do this in the following way:

```
print("Learning Python is fun")
```

```
print('Learning Python is fun')
```

```
print("""Learning Python is fun""")
```

Executing the above command in your terminal windows gives the same output as displayed below:

```
Learning Python is fun
```

Python Backslash

It is a good practice to keep the number of lines in your code to a maximum length of 79 characters. If your code exceeds this limit of 79 characters, you can insert a backslash statement and continue the code on the next line. Let us see an example:

```
def print_sentence():
    sentence = 'Hello! Python is a beautiful language. Would you
like to master this beautiful language?' + \
               'Type y for Yes or n for
    No' print(sentence)
```

In the function print_sentence, we have extended the line which includes the sentence by inserting the backslash or \ character. Python internally understands that it is part of the same line, but this makes the code more readable and follows best practices. The output of the function after calling it is as follows:

```
Hello! Python is a beautiful language. Would you like to master
this beautiful language?Type y for Yes or n for No
```

Strings inside the quotes

We already saw how we can print a string by using a single quote, or a double-quote. But, how can we print a quote within a string? We can use a single quote or a double quote to embed a quote within a string.

```
print("Hello 'World'")
```

```
print('Hello "World"')
```

The above two code snippets show the two ways to include a quote within a string. The output of both the code snippets is as follows:

```
Hello 'World'
```

The Escape Sequence

Escape sequences are used to print special characters like inverted commas, backslashes, etc. in your string. Let us look at a few examples:

```
sentence = "What\'s new in Python3.8?"
print(sentence)
```

In order to print the apostrophe mark, we need to use the "\" symbol before the apostrophe mark. The output of the print command is as follows:

```
What's new in Python3.8?
```

New Line

In order to display a new line in your string, we need to use "\n" to indicate the beginning of a new line. Let us look at an example.

```
sentence = "There are many programming languages.\nPython is
considered to be the most flexible programming language"
```

In the output below, we see that the sentence or the string could be split into two separate lines.

```
There are many programming languages.
Python is considered to be the most flexible programming language
```

Horizontal tab

The horizontal tab character also indicated with the “\t” symbol is used to include spaces or tabs in your string. Let us look at an example:

```
value = "Python\tC++"
```

On printing the value variable, we get the following output:

```
Python	C++
```

String Concatenation

Oftentimes you would have two or more strings or words, and you would like to concatenate them together. We can use the + operator to concatenate two strings. Let us see an example:

```
language = "Python"
sentence = "is a beautiful language"
output = language + sentence
print(output)
```

The output after concatenating Python and is a beautiful language is as follows. We could replace the string Python with any other language and would get the appropriate output.

```
Python is a beautiful language
```

Let us replace the word Python with C++ and see the output:

```
language = "C++"
sentence = "is a beautiful language"
output = language + sentence
```

```
print(output)
```

The output of the above code snippet is as follows:

```
C++ is a beautiful language
```

Indentation

Unlike other programming languages, Python uses indentation not only for code readability but also for creating blocks of code. For example, if you use a while or for loop, it is important to use 4 spaces of indentation for the inner block of the code. In the example below, we have a function to check if the number given as an argument to the function is even or odd. There is one indentation below the function name to indicate the start of a new block, and another indentation within the if and else block.

```
def is_even(number):
    if number %2 == 0:
        print({} is even.format(number))
    else:
        print({} is odd.format(number))
```

Exercise

1. Write a program to print your name and age.
2. Print your name and where you come from on two different lines.

NOTES

Chapter 3: Variables

What is a variable?

Imagine you have a big family. Each family member gets a unique name. Just how humans address other humans and inanimate objects by names, you have to address a block of memory by a variable name. Let us see how this works in detail.

We will take the example of naming colors and addressing those colors by unique variable names.

Let us imagine we are developing a paint application, and we would like to implement a feature where the user can select different colors. Let us take 4 colors for this example - orange, red, green, blue. In order to represent this in a programming language like Python, we need unique variables. We will store the color orange indicated by the variable 'a', the color red indicated by the variable 'b', the color green indicated by the variable 'c' and the color yellow indicated by the variable 'd'.

```
a = 'orange'
b = 'red'
c = 'green'
d = 'yellow'
```

Let us now print the value of the variable 'a'. You can execute the following command in your terminal window.

```
print(a)
```

You get the following output:

```
orange
```

Let us now change the value of variable 'a' to 'purple'.

```
a = 'purple'
```

```
print(a)
```

The output of the print(a) command is as follows:

```
purple
```

You can see that the variable ‘a’ was overwritten and ‘a’ now holds the value ‘purple’ instead of ‘orange’.

In the above example, we have explored that a variable can store a string value. In the next sections, we will learn about different data types and how to store them in a variable.

Rules to name variables in Python

In Python, there are certain conventions to be followed while naming variables. In this section, we will look at some ways to name variables.

1. You should name the variables starting with a character or an underscore sign.
2. You should never name variables starting with a number.
3. Variable names should contain alphanumeric characters only.
4. Variable names are case-sensitive, i.e. age and Age would be considered as two unique variable names.

Let us look at some examples to name variables.

```
language_programming = 'Python'
_programmingLanguage = 'Python'
programmingLanguage1 = 'Python'
```

The above three variable names are valid variable names. They consist of alphanumeric characters, underscore sign and does not begin with a number. Now let us look at some incorrect ways to name variables.

```
1programming_language = 'Python'
$programmingLanguage = 'Python'
```

In the above example, the variable names begin with a number and a $ sign, which is not allowed in Python. Naming the variables in this way would lead to a syntax error.

Variable Assignments

Setting a value to a variable is known as a variable assignment. In this section, we will look at some ways of assigning a value to a variable. We already looked at how to set a string value to a variable in the first section of this chapter.

You can assign a value to a variable using the "=" operator. The value on the right-hand side of the operator is set to the variable name on the left-hand side of the operator.

```
variable_name = value
```

There are two ways to set a value to a variable. Let us explore these two ways in this section.

Single Assignment

Single assignment is the traditional way of setting values. For example:

a = 100 will set the variable a to a value of 100.

Multiple Assignment

Let us say you want to set the same value to two or more variables. In this scenario, you would set the value as follows:

a1 = b1 = c1 = 100

In the above example, the variables a1, b1, and c1 hold the value 100.
Let us now see how these variables are stored in memory. We can print the address of the variable using the id function that comes in - built with Python.

```
print(id(a1), id(b1), id(c1))
```

```
94642424905856 94642424905856 94642424905856
```

We can observe that all variables point to the same memory address in memory. Let us now change the value of a1 to 12 and print their memory address again.

```
a1 = 12
print(id(a1), id(b1), id(c1))
```

We observe that the address of a1 has changed but both b1 and c1 still point to the same memory address.

```
94642424903040 94642424905856 94642424905856
```

Data Types in a variable

In the previous section, we explored how we can set a value to a variable name. We explored the string data type. In this section, we will discuss what is a data type and the different data types Python support.

In programming, there are various ways to model a business problem into actual code. To model a number, we need an equivalent type in Python. Similarly to model characters, strings, decimals, etc. we need appropriate types in Python. Unlike a statically typed language, Python is a dynamically typed language, i.e. once a variable is defined we can change its type by setting the corresponding value. Let us look at an example:

```
a = 10
```

We can get the type by using the type function.

```
print(type(a))
```

We get the following output:

```
<class 'int'>
```

Let us now change the value of a.

```
a = 'Python'
```

```
print(type(a))
```

We get the following output after changing the value of *a* from *10* to *Python:*

```
<class 'str'>
```

As you can see, variables can hold different data types, which makes Python easy to use.

There are 5 Python data types:

1. Numbers
2. Strings
3. Tuples
4. List
5. Dictionary

Numbers

Numbers can be categorized under integer and floating-point numbers. An integer is a whole number, i.e. it holds negative and positive numbers including 0. A floating -point number is a decimal number, i.e. it holds fractions. Let us look at an example of an integer and a floating-point number.

```
a = 128
print(type(a))
```

The output of the type function of the variable a with value 128 is int, as indicated below:

```
<class 'int'>
```

Let us now change the value of a from 128 to 128.0 indicating that it is no more an integer but a decimal number.

```
a = 128.0
print(type(a))
```

The output of the type function in the above case would be as follows:

```
<class 'float'>
```

Integers are whole numbers starting such as 0,1,2,3, etc. Since integer numbers are whole numbers, they don't hold decimal values. Integers can be both negative and positive.

Floating-point numbers are characterized by decimal numbers of fraction numbers. There are two ways to represent a floating-point number:

a. Decimal representation like 5.44 or 6.879576
b. Scientific notation, like 5.38e7

The *e* in the scientific notation means how many places the decimal would move to the right. 5.38e7 in decimal representation would be 5.38 x 10^7 or 53800000.0.

Strings

We already saw an example of the string data type. Strings can be represented with double or single inverted commas. For example:

```
language = 'Python'
print(type(language))
language = "Python"
print(type(language))
```

The output of the type command is as follows. We can see that the variable language is of type str or string.

```
<class 'str'>
<class 'str'>
```

Complex Numbers

A complex number is represented by a real part and an imaginary part. A complex number is represented mathematically in the following form

a + bj,

where 'a' is the real part and 'b' is the imaginary part.

Let's see how we can create a complex number in Python:

```
complex_number = complex(12,5)
print(type(complex_number))
```

The output of the type function is as follows. The number is represented as a complex data type.

```
<class 'complex'>
```

Let us now see how can we extract the real and imaginary parts of a complex number:

```
a = complex_numer.real
b = complex_number.imag
print('Real number is {}'.format(a))
print('Imaginary number is {}'.format(b))
```

We get the output of the above two print commands as follows.

```
Real number is 12.0
Imaginary number is 5.0
```

In order to extract the real and imaginary numbers, we can use the real and image property of the complex number.

Deleting a variable

In some instances, you might want to delete a variable to free up memory. You can use the del operator to delete a variable from the memory. Let us see an example:

```
x_mean = 12
print(x_mean)
```

Let us now see the output of x_mean. As you can see below, the python interpreter prints the value 12 since x_mean is holding the value 12.

```
12
```

Let us now use the del keyword to delete the variable x_mean from the memory.

```
del x_mean
print(x_mean)
```

When we now print x_mean, we get the following output. The output is as follows:

```
Traceback (most recent call last):
  File "<stdin>", line 1, in <module>
NameError: name 'x_mean' is not defined
```

Since x_mean was deleted, when we access the variable again, we get an error.

Reserved Keywords

Python has some built-in keywords which should not be used as variable names. Let us look at these keywords:

1. False
2. True
3. None
4. and
5. as
6. assert
7. break
8. class
9. continue
10. def
11. if
12. elif
13. else
14. del
15. except
16. finally
17. for
18. from
19. globally
20. import
21. in
22. is
23. lambda
24. nonlocal
25. not
26. or
27. pass
28. raise
29. return
30. try
31. while
32. with
33. yield

You will learn some of these keywords over the new few chapters.

Exercise

In this exercise drill, we will implement a book inventory application and print some important details of the book in our inventory. Imagine you own a library and your small library has 100 books. Out of those 100 books, you have lent 50 books. You need to print the books owned by the library, the books lent out to your members, and books still available in your inventory.

```
number_of_books = 100
books_lent = 50
remaining_books = number_of_books - books_lent

print('Our library has {} books'.format(number_of_books))
print('Our library has lent {} books'.format(books_lent))
print('Our library has {} books available to be
read'.format(remaining_books))
```

Let us observe the output:

```
Our library has 100 books
Our library has lent 50 books
Our library has 50 books available to be read
```

We have declared three variables number_of_books, books_lent, and remaining_books, and assigned them appropriate values as stated in the question. We then print the information related to our library.

NOTES

Chapter 4: Operators for Variables

What are operators?

Operators are special symbols that can perform a mathematical operation on a variable. There are different types of operators and in this section we will have a look at those operators and how to use them in Python.

There are 5 types of operators:

1. Arithmetic Operators
2. Assignment Operators
3. Comparison Operators
4. Membership Operators
5. Bitwise Operators
6. Logical Operators
7. Identity Operators

Arithmetic Operators

Assignment operators as the name suggests are used to assign values to variables. Let us look at some examples of Arithmetic Operators in this section.

1. Addition Operator +

An addition operator is used to increment the value of a variable by a given number. It is denoted by the + sign. Let us look at an example of an addition operator:

```
number = 0
number = number + 1
print(number)
```

We have defined a variable called number and initialized it with the value 0. In order to increment the value of 'number' by 1, we use the '+' operator. Let us now look at the output of the print command below.

```
1
```

2. Subtraction Operator

The subtraction operator is used to decrement the value of a variable by a given number. It is denoted by the - symbol.

```
number = 0
number = number - 1
print(number)
```

The result of the above statement would be -1

3. Multiplication Operator

The multiplication operator is used to multiply two or more numbers. Let us look at an example of multiplying two numbers. The multiplication operator is denoted by the "*" symbol.

```
a = 5
b = 12
result = a * b
print(result)
```

The result of the above operation would be 60.

4. Division Operator

The division operator as the name suggests is used to divide two numbers. The division operator is denoted by the "/" symbol or the "//" symbol. When we want the result of division to round to a whole number, then we should use the "//" symbol.

```
a = 24
```

```
b = 6
result = a/b
print(result)
```

The result of 24/6 would be 4.0

```
a = 24
b = 6
result = a//b
print(result)
```

The result of 24//6 would be 4.

5. Modulus Operator

The modulus operator is used to find the remainder of two integers. Let us see an example.

```
a = 25
b = 2
result = a%b
print(result)
```

In the above code snippet, when we divide 25 by 2 the remainder would be 1 which would be the output of the modulus operator.

6. Exponentiation or power operator

The exponentiation operator is used to take the power of two numbers.
The exponentiation operator is denoted by the "**" symbol.

```
a=5
b=3
result = a**b
print(result)
```

In the above example, the power of 5 raised to 3 is 125 which is the output of the exponentiation operator.

Assignment Operator

Assignment operators are used to assign values to a variable. We already saw an example of an assignment operator at the beginning of the chapter. An assignment operator in its simplest form can be denoted by the "=" symbol. In this section, we will look at some other assignment operators.

We will define a variable x and initialize it with a value of 0.

```
x = 0
```

We can combine the arithmetic operators such as +, -, *, /, //, %, **, etc. to form compound operators. Let us have a look at some examples of these compound operators:

1. "+="

The "+=" operator is used to increment the value of a variable by a given number and assign the variable the incremented value.

```
x += 1
```

In the above example, x is incremented by 1, and it holds the value 1.

2. "-=" operator

The "-=" operator is used to decrement the value of a variable by a given number and assign the variable the decremented value.

```
x = 0
x-= 1
print(x)
```

The output of the above example would be -1 since before decrementing the value of x by 1 x was initialized to hold the value 0. After decrementing and assigning the value of x by 1 the result of x would be -1. The output x-=1 is equivalent to x = x-1.

3. "*=" operator

The "*=" operator or the multiplicative and assignment operator is used to multiply a variable by a number and assigning the variable the output of the multiplication. Let us see an example:

```
x = -1
x *= -1
print(x)
```

The statement x *= -1 is equivalent to x = x*-1. Initially, x held the value -1. The multiplication and assignment operator changes the value of x from -1 to 1 since -1*-1=1.

4. "/=" operator

The "/=" operator is used to divide a number by another number and setting the variable with the resulting value. Let us say we have a variable x and would like to divide x by 3 i.e. x/3. This can be written as follows x /=3 which is equivalent to x = x/3.

```
x = 5
x /= 3
print(x)
```

The output of the above command would be 1.6666666666666667.

5. "//=" operator.

The "//=" operator ensures the output of dividing a number by another is always a whole number. Taking the same example as the previous one, the output of x//=3 would be 1 since 1.6666666666666667 round off to the nearest whole number is 1.

6. "%=" operator

The "%=" operator is used to take the remaining of a number and store the resulting output in the same variable. Let us see an example:

```
x = 5
x%=2
```

```
print(x)
```

The statement x%=2 is equivalent to x = x%2 i.e. nothing but 5%2 which is equal to 1.

7. "**=" operator

The "**=" operator is used to take the power of a number and assign the resulting value to the same variable. Let us see an example:

```
x = 25
x**=3
print(x)
```

The output of the above command would be 15625 since x**=3 is equivalent to x=x**3. Since x is 25 the output of 25^3 is 15625.

Comparison Operator

Comparison Operators are logical operators, and the output of these operators is either True or False. They are also known as boolean operators. Let us look at some examples of these operators:

1. "==" operator

The "==" operator is used to compare two variables. If the variables are equal the output would be True and if they are not equal the output would be False. Let us look at an example:

```
language1 = "Python"
language2 = "C++"
isSame = language1 == language2
print(isSame)
```

In the above example, we have created two variables -- language1 and language2. They both have different values, so the == operator would return False. Let us now change the value of language2= "Python" and see the output:

```
language1 = "Python"
language2 = "Python"
isSame == language1 == language2
print(isSame)
```

The output of the variable isSame would be True since both language1 and language2 hold the same string value, i.e. "Python."

2. ">" operator

The ">" operator is used to compare if the left hand side value is strictly greater than the right-hand side value. Let us see an example:

```
a = 12
b = 14
isGreater = a > b
print(isGreater)
a = 15
print(isGreater)
```

In the above code snippet, we first initialize a and b to hold the values 12 and 14 respectively. The output, in this case, would be False since 12 < 14. On changing the value of a to be 15 the output would be True since 15 > 14.

3. "<" operator

The "<" operator is used to compare if the left-hand side value is strictly less than the right-hand side value.

```
a = 12
b = 14
isSmaller = a < b
print(isSmaller)
```

In the above code snippet, the output would be True since 12 < 14.

4. ">=" operator

The ">=" operator is used to compare if the left hand side value is greater than or equal to the right-hand side value.

```
a = 12
b = 12
isGreaterEqual = a >=b
print(isGreaterEqual)
```

The ">=" will check if the value of the variable a is either greater than b or equal to the variable. If one of these conditions is met, the output of the operator will be True. In the above code snippet, since 12==12 the output would be True.

5. "<=" operator

The "<=" operator is used to compare if the left-hand side value is less than or equal to the right-hand side value.

```
a = 12
b = 12
isLessEqual =  a <=b
print(isLessEqual)
```

Following the logic of the ">=" operator, the "<=" operator will return True if the value of the variable a is either less than b or equal to b. In the above code snippet, since both a and b are equal, the output would be True.

6. “!=” operator

The “!=” operator is used to compare if the left-hand side value is not equal to the right-hand side value. If the two values are not equal the comparison operator it will return True whereas if they are not equal, the output of the operator will be False.

```
a = 1
b = 2
isNotEqual = a!=b
```

Unlike the equality operator, the “!’=” operator will return True if the value of the variables a and b are not equal. In the above example, since 1!=2 the output would be True.

Logical Operator

Logical operators derive their name from logical gates AND, OR, and NOT. It is used to do a logical comparison between the operands. Let us explore the three logical operators in detail.

1. AND operator

The logical AND operator is used to do a logical AND between the operands. In order to understand the AND operator, let us first have a look at the truth table of the AND operation.

a	b	a AND b
True	True	True
True	False	False
False	True	False
False	False	False

Let us now see the AND operator in action. Imagine you are given a variable with a value between 1 and 100, and you want to check if the value is greater than 5 and less than 10. We can solve this problem using the AND operator.

```
x = 7
a = x>5
b = x < 10
result = a and b
print(result)
```

The output of the above code snippet would be True since a = x>5 would return True because 7>5 and b would also return True since b=x<10 would be 7<10 which is True. Since a is True and b is also True, the output would be True and True, which according to the truth table is True.

2. OR operator

The logical OR operator is used to do a logical OR between the operands. In order to understand the OR operator, let us first have a look at the truth table of the OR operation.

a	b	a OR b
True	True	True
True	False	True
False	True	True
False	False	False

Let us now see the OR operator in action. Imagine you are given a variable with a value between 1 and 100, and you want to check if the value is either less than 5 or greater than 10. We can solve this problem using the OR operator.

```
x = 3
a = x < 5
b = x > 10
result = a or b
```

```
x = 12
a = x  < 5
b = x > 10
result = a or b
```

Let us initialize a variable x with the value 3. The variable *a* will be the output of the "<" comparison operator i.e. the output of 3 < 5 and the variable b will be the output of the ">" comparison operator i.e. the output of 3 > 10. Since 3 < 5 the variable a will be True and since 3>10 is not True the variable b will be False. The result would be True or False, which according to the truth table of the OR logic is True. We can now change the value of x from 3 to 12, and we would get the same output. The only difference would be that a would compute to False and b to True.

3. NOT operator

The NOT is an inversion operator. To understand the NOT operator, let us have a look at the truth table of the NOT operator.

a	NOT A
True	False
False	True

Let us now look at an example:

```
x = False
result = not x
print(result)
```

The output of the above code snippet would be True since x is False and the inversion of False which is indicated by not x is always True.

Identity Operator

The identity operator is used to check if the variables are stored in the same part of the memory or not. There are two types of Identity operators -- the *is* operator and the *is not* operator.

1. is operator

```
a = 12
b = a
result  = a is b
print(result)
print(id(a))
print(id(b))
```

```
True
94785170621824
94785170621824
```

2. is not operator

```
b = 14
result =  a is not b
print(result)
print(id(a))
print(id(b))
```

```
False
94785170621824
94785170621920
```

Membership Operator

1. in operator

The in operator is used to check if a value is present in a list or a string. For example, in the example below, we would like to check if the word “Python” is present in the sentence “Python is a wonderful language.”

```
sentence = "Python is a wonderful language"
result = "Python" in sentence
```

The output after executing the above code would be True, since “Python” is indeed present in the sentence.

2. not in operator

The not in operator is to check for the absence of a word or value in a string or a list.

```
sentence = "Python is a wonderful language"
result = "C++" not in sentence
print(result)
```

The output of the above code snippet would be True, since “C++” is not there in the sentence.

Bitwise Operator

In this section, we will look at Bitwise operators. In the previous section, we already had a look and the AND operation and the OR operation. In this section, we look at how to perform bitwise and, or, xor, and bitwise left and right shift.

1. & operator

The “&” operator is used to perform a bitwise and operation.

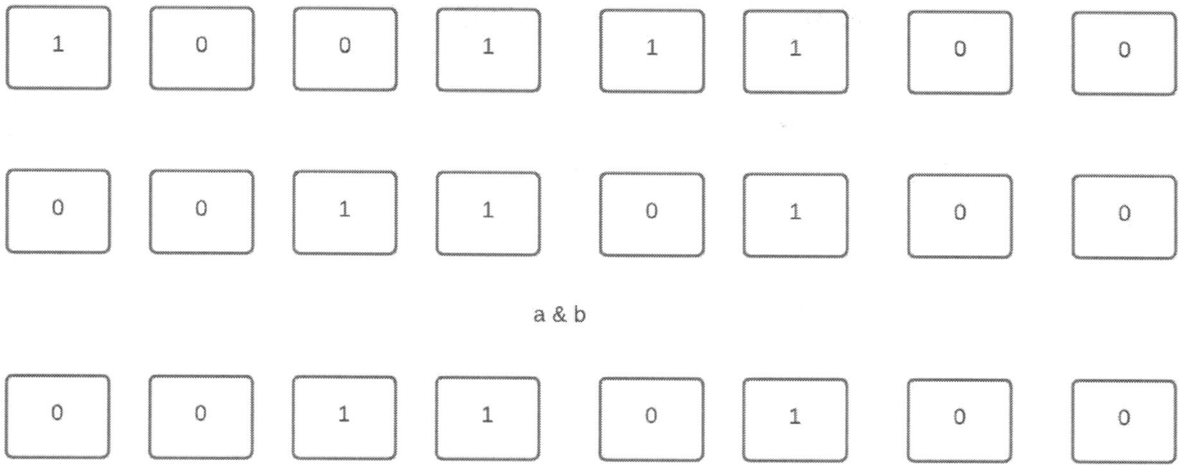

In the above example, we have two binary numbers. Let us denote a by 10011100 and b by 00110100. When we do a bit-wise and operation, the output would be set to 1 when both a and b are one, otherwise the output bit would be set to 0.

2. | operator

The "|" operator is also known as the bit-wise or operator. Let us look at an example.

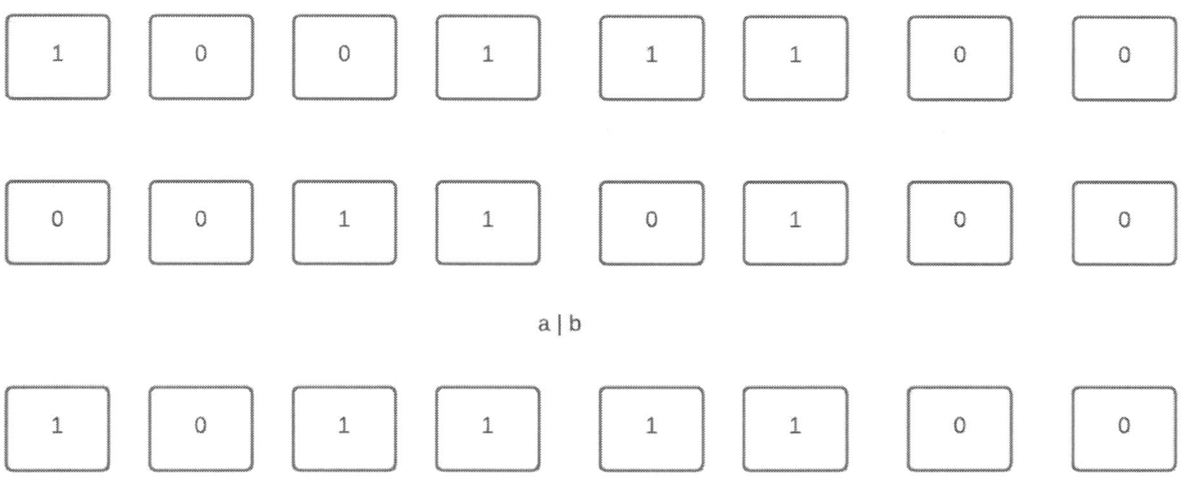

In the above example, we have two binary numbers. Let us denote a by 10011100 and b by 00110100. When we do a bit-wise or operation, the output would be set to 1 when either a is 1 or b is one or both a and b are 1. If both a and b are 0 then the output would be set to 0.

3. ~ operator

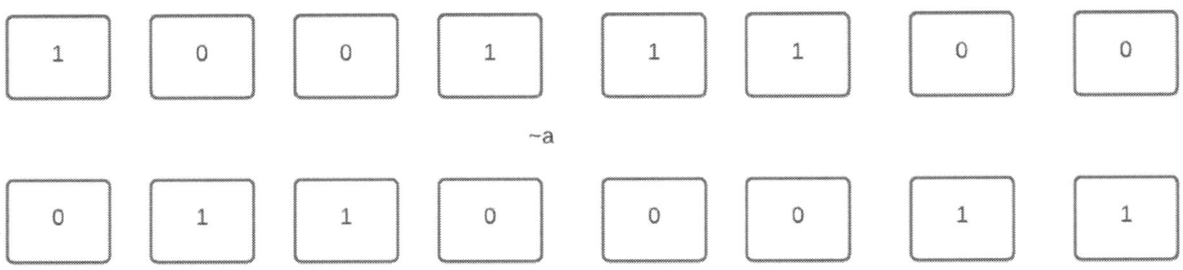

The negation operator simply inverts the bit, i.e. 1 becomes 0 and 0 becomes 1.

4. ^ operator

The "^" operator is also known as the xor operator. Let us see an example:

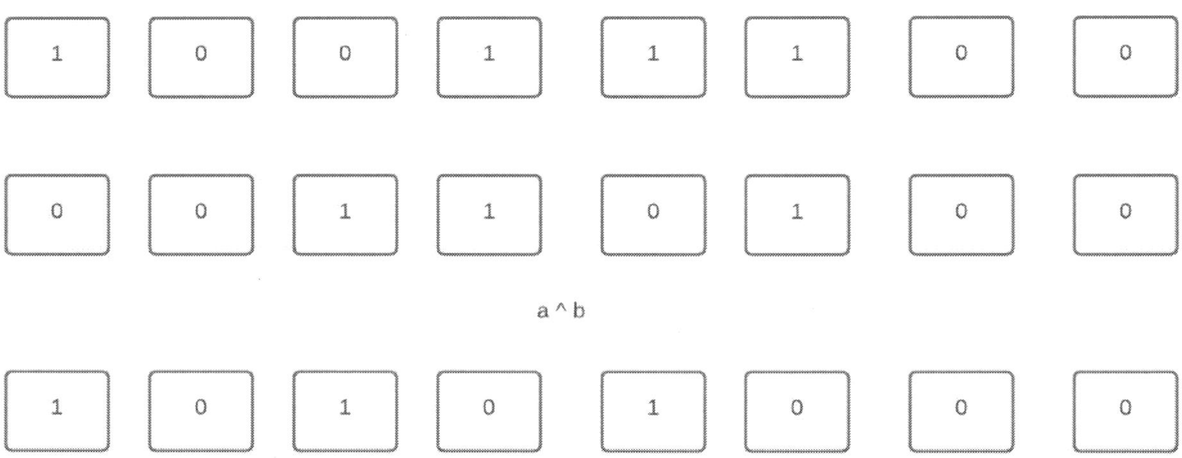

In the above example, we have two binary numbers. Let us denote a by 10011100 and b by 00110100. When we do a bit-wise xor operation, the output would be set to 1 when either a is 1 and b is 0 or a is 0 and b is 1. In any other case i.e. when both a and b have the same values then the output would be set to 0.

5. >> operator

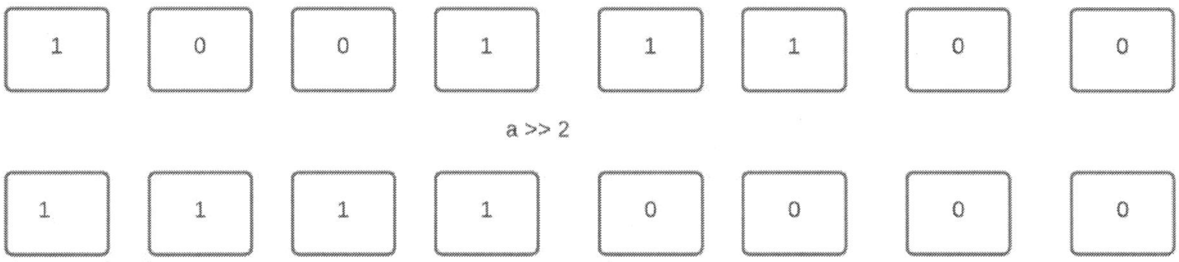

The right shift operator denoted by “>>” is used to multiply a number by a power of 2. In the above example, *a* is represented by 00111100 which is the binary representation of the number 60 and when we do a right shift by 2 the output would be 60 *2 * 2 which is 240, and in binary representation 11110000.

6. << operator

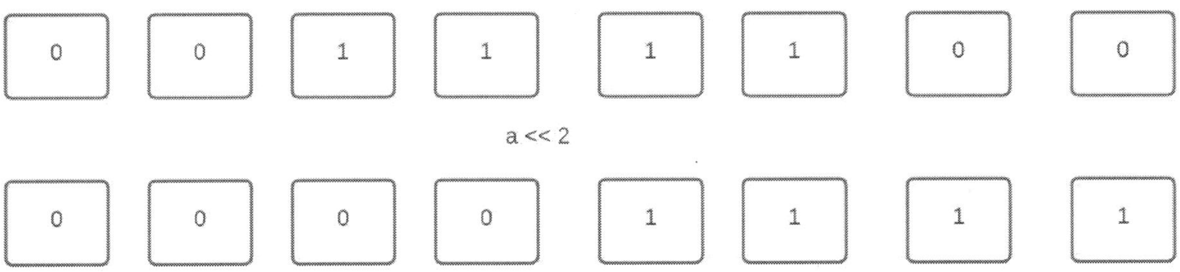

The left shift operator denoted by “<<” is used to divide a number by a power of 2. In the above example, a is represented by 00111100 which is the binary representation of the number 60 and when we do a left shift by 2 the output would be 60 /4 which is 15 and in binary representation 11110000.

Exercise Drill

1. Given three numbers, write a program to find the sum of the three numbers.

```
a = 12
b = 13
c = 14
result = a+b+c
print(result)
```

```
39
```

2. Given a list of countries, find out if USA is present in the list.

```
countries = ['UK', 'Germany', 'USA', 'Japan']
isCountry = 'USA' in countries
print(isCountry)
```

Output

```
True
```

NOTES

Chapter 5: Strings

What are strings?

Strings are nothing but a sequence or a list of characters. Let us take an example of a string and see how it is represented in the memory of your computer.

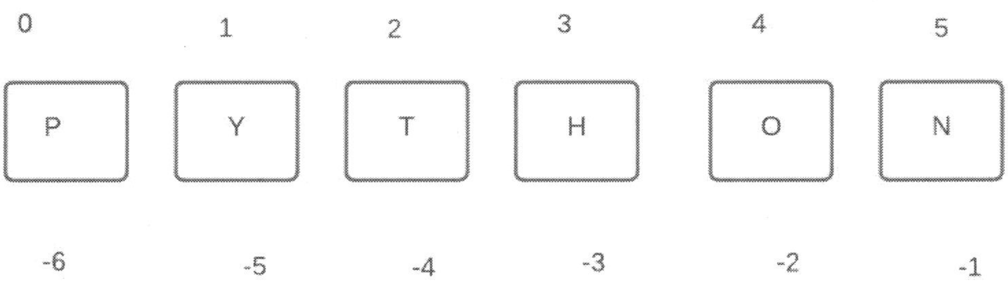

In the above example, we see the string Python represented as an array of characters.

An array starts at the 0th index. Let us see how we can access individual characters from a string

```
word = "Python"
print(word[0])
print(word[3])
```

Since ‘P’ is at the 0th index and ‘h’ at the 3rd index, we get the following output.

```
'P'
'h'
```

How to use Strings?

We can represent a string using either a single quotation mark or a double quotation mark

```
word = 'Python'
print(word)
word = "Python"
print(word)
```

Using either a single or a double quotation mark does not make a difference to the output.

```
Python
Python
```

Types of Strings

There are two types of strings -- the single-line string and the multi-line string. Let us discuss both these types in detail.

Single Line Strings

A single line string is represented by a double quotation mark and spans the length of a line.

```
a = "Goodbye"
print(a)
```

In the above code snippet, we have assigned the value “Goodbye” to the variable *a*. Since it spans only one line, we can use the double quotation mark. The output is as follows:

```
Goodbye
```

Multi-line Strings

If the string spans more than one line, we can use the triple quotation mark. Let us have a look at an example:

```
a = """Hello everyone in the world, this is a \
message to all the Python users."""
print(a)
```

We get the following output:

```
'Hello everyone in the world, this is a message to all the Python
users.'
```

String Concatenation

Imagine you are given two strings and would like to merge the value of the two strings in one string variable. We can concatenate two strings using the "+" operator. Let us look at an example:

```
language = "Python"
feature = "easy to learn"
result = language + " is " + feature
print(result)
```

```
'Python is easy to learn'
```

In the above example, the variable result stores the concatenation of the strings "Python", "is" and "easy to learn."

Details of Strings

Length of a String

The length of a string represents the total number of characters in a string. We can get the length of a string by the in -built *len* method.

```
a = "Python"
n = len(a)
print(n)
a = "Hello World"
n = len(a)
print(n)
```

The word Python has 6 alphabets or characters, whereas the string “Hello World” has 10 letters and an empty space. The output of the length of the string “Python” would be 6 whereas the output for the word “Hello World” would be 10+1=11.

```
6
11
```

Looping

Since the string is an array of characters, we can loop through the string and access individual characters. Let us see an example:

```
sentence = "hello world"
for char in sentence:
    print(char)
```

We loop through the sentence “hello world” and at every iteration we access the character at a particular index. The loop runs from index 0 to the length of the string. The output is as follows:

```
h
e
l
l
```

```
o
 
w
o
r
l
d
```

Converting a string from lower-case to upper-case

In many text based processing tasks, you might have to convert a string from lower-case to upper-case or vice-versa. Let us look at an example how we can achieve this.

```
language = "PYTHON"
print(language.lower())
language = "python"
print(language.upper())
```

```
python
PYTHON
```

We can use the upper() and lower() method to convert string from one case to another.

Check if a word is present in a string

While working with strings or sentences, you might want to check if a word is present in a string or not. We can use the in operator to check for the presence or absence of a word. Let us look at an example:

```
txt = "I want to travel the world"
result = "world" in txt
print(result)
```

```
True
```

We can also use an if statement to check if a word exists in a sentence or not. Let us see an example:

```
txt = "I want to travel the world"
query_word = "world"
if query_word in txt:
    print("The query word {} is present in the
sentence".format(query_word))
```

In the above code snippet, we have a query word “word” and we would like to check if the query word is present in the string “txt” or not. We have used a conditional if statement to check for the word and if the condition is met, the print statement would be executed. The output is as follows:

```
The query word world is present in the sentence
```

Check if a word is not present in a string

We can also check for the absence of a word using the not in operator. Let us have a look at an example:

```
txt = "I want to travel the world"
query_word = "Paris"
if query_word not in txt:
    print("The query word {} is not present in
the sentence".format(query_word))
```

In the above code snippet, we have a query word “Paris” and we would like to check if the query word is present in the string “txt” or not. We have u sed a conditional if statement to check for the absence of the word and if the condition is met, the print statement would be executed. The output is as follows:

```
The query word Paris is not present in the sentence
```

Assignment

1. Write a program to find the 3rd character in the string “Hello World.”
2. Write a program to iterate over the string “Python is a beautiful language” and print each character of the string on a new line.

NOTES

Chapter 6: Tuples, List, and Dictionary

In this chapter, we will learn about some additional data structures like tuples, lists, and dictionaries. As you progress in learning Python, these data structures will become very important. Let us begin our discussion by introducing the concept of tuples.

Tuple

A tuple is used to store many items of different data types addressed by a single variable. Let us look at an example.

Let us imagine we need to have an application that renders the names of different fruits. Instead of addressing each fruit with a separate variable name, we can store them in a single variable.

```
fruits = ("Apples", "Pears", "Melon", "Grapes")
```

Properties of Tuples

1. Ordered

A tuple, unlike a dictionary, which we will discuss in the next sections, stores the data in the order they were created.

```
print(fruits[0])
print(fruits[1])
print(fruits[2])
print(fruits[3])
```

In the above code-snippet, we see that the first element in the tuple is "Apples" since this was the first fruit that was created. Similarly, all the remaining fruits are printed in the order they were created.

```
'Apples'
```

```
'Pears'
'Fruits'
'Grapes'
```

2. Immutability

Another interesting property of a tuple is immutability, i.e. a tuple once created cannot change its value. Let us see what happens when we try to change the value of the first index in a tuple.

```
fruits[0] = "Mango"
```

The above statement will lead to an error as shown below.

```
Traceback (most recent call last):
  File "<stdin>", line 1, in <module>
TypeError: 'tuple' object does not support item assignment
```

3. Duplicate Elements

A tuple supports adding duplicate elements. Let us see an example:

```
fruits = ("Apples", "Pears", "Melon", "Grapes", "Apples")
```

In the above example, we have inserted “Apples” twice. Let us now print fruits and see the result.

```
('Apples', 'Pears', 'Melon', 'Grapes', 'Apples')
```

We can see that the tuple was created with two apples, and they were inserted in the order that they were created. This is in contrast to a set that allows inserting only unique elements and removes duplicate elements.

List

A list is one of the most fundamental and important data structure in any programming language. In this section, we will see how to create a list and perform some common operations on it. A list is nothing but a collection of items. Let us create a list with names of different Programming languages

```
languages = ["Python", "C++", "Ruby", "Java"]
```

In the above code snippet, we have created a list using the square bracket [ ] and the list is addressed by the variable languages. We can get the number of elements in a list using the *len* method.

```
len(languages)
```

We get the following output:

```
4
```

Properties of Lists

1. Lists are ordered. Just like tuples, lists store elements in the order that they were created. Let us print the very first element in the list by executing the following command on your Python shell.

   ```
   print(languages[0])
   ```

   We get the following output

   ```
   Python
   ```

   Since Python was the very first element that was created, the list preserves this order.

2. Mutability

Lists unlike tuples are mutable, i.e. the elements within a list can be changed at any point in time. Let us replace "Ruby" with "Swift". We can do this as follows:

```
languages[2] = "Swift"
```

```
print(languages)
```

```
['Python', 'C++', 'Swift', 'Java']
```

3. Inserting an element in a list

We can insert new elements in a list using the append method.

```
languages.append("Python")
print(languages)
```

```
['Python', 'C++', 'Swift', 'Java', 'Python']
```

In the above example, we have appended a new element to the list. Lists can include duplicate elements.

Dictionary

A dictionary is a data structure used to store key value elements. A dictionary cannot have duplicate keys and just like lists are immutable and be modified. Let us look at an example.

Let us imagine an application where we need to count the number of fruits we have purchased. A dictionary would be an appropriate data structure in this scenario.

A dictionary is created using curly brackets {} or the dict keyword.

```
fruits = {'Apples': 2, 'Lemon': 1, 'Pears':
2} print(type(fruits))
```

```
<class 'dict'>
```

We can access all the unique keys of the dictionary and the corresponding values using the keys() and values() method, respectively.

```
print(fruits.keys())
print(fruits.values())
```

```
dict_keys(['Apples', 'Lemon', 'Pears'])
dict_values([2, 1, 2])
```

If we want to access the value of a specific key, we can do this using square brackets.

```
print(fruits['Apples'])
```

```
2
```

We can update the value of a specific key as follows:

```
fruits['Apples'] = 5
print(fruits)
```

```
{'Apples': 5, 'Lemon': 1, 'Pears': 2}
```

We can insert a new key, value pair using the update method.

```
fruit = {'Mango': 3}
fruits.update(fruit)
print(fruits)
```

```
{'Apples': 5, 'Lemon': 1, 'Pears': 2, 'Mango': 3}
```

We can get the length of the dictionary using the *len* keyword.

```
print(len(fruits))
```

```
4
```

NOTES

Chapter 7: Statements and Loops

In this chapter, we will learn about statements and loops. Learning about different types of loops like if else, while loops will help you write better code and make things easier.

Statements

We have already discussed the concept of a statement when we discussed Variables in Chapter 2. A statement is a line of code that can assign a value to a variable, initialize a list, dictionary, tuple etc. or jump from one part of the code to another using functions which we will discuss in the next Chapter.

```
a = 12
years = [2018, 2019, 2021]
```

In the above example, the line a= 12 is a statement that stores the value of 12 in a variable called 'a'. The statement years = [2018, 2019, 2021] initializes the list years with 3 elements.

Loops

Loops are used to iterate over a range of values. We can use loop to iterate over lists, dictionary, tuples etc. There are two types of loops - a for loop and a while loop. Let us look at an example of both in the next section.
Let us print the value of the first 10 numbers using a loop.

```
for x in range(1,11):
    print(x)
```

```
1
2
3
4
5
6
7
8
9
```

```
10
```

In the above example, we have used the range function to generate a list of numbers from 1 to 11. We can then iterate over these numbers using the for loop.. At every iteration, we print the value of x.

Break Statement

We can use the break keyword to stop the for loop. In the example below, if the number is greater than 5 the program will exit the for loop and continue with the rest of the program.

```
for x in range(1,11):
    if x > 5:
        break
    print(x)
```

The output is as follows:

```
1
2
3
4
5
```

Continue Statement

The 'continue' keyword is used to skip an iteration based on some condition. In the example below, we will again print the numbers from 1 to 10 but when x is 5 the program will skip the iteration and continue with the remaining iterations.

```
for x in range(1, 11):
    if x==5:
        continue
    print(x)
```

The output is as follows:

```
1
2
3
```

```
4
6
7
8
9
10
```

We can observe that the number 5 was never printed.

Else Statement

We can use the else statement to gracefully exit the for loop. Let us look at an example:

```
for x in range(1,11):
    print(x)
else:
   print('Loop ends')
```

We can see in the output once the program finished printing the numbers 1 to 10, the program jumps to the else block and prints 'Loop ends'.

```
1
2
3
4
5
6
7
8
9
10
Loop ends
```

Nested Loop

We can use a nested loop to run an inner loop within an outer loop. In the example below the x iterates over the adj list which consists of the adjectives "red", "big", and "tasty and for every x value another loop is executed which iterates over the fruits array which consists of "apple", "banana", and "cherry".

```
adj = ["red", "big", "tasty"]
fruits = ["apple", "banana", "cherry"]
for x in adj:
    for  y in fruits:
        print(x,y)
```

```
red apple
red banana
red cherry
big apple
big banana
big cherry
tasty apple
tasty banana
tasty cherry
```

As you can see from the output above, the program prints the fruit name for every adjective.

While Loop

A while loop is used to run a block of code within the while loop until a certain logical condition is satisfied. If there is no terminating condition, the while loop will run infinitely.

```
x = 10
while x > 0:
    print(x)
    x = x-1
```

```
10
9
```

```
8
7
6
5
4
3
2
1
```

In the example above, the value of x is initially set to 10. The while loop runs the block of code as long as the value of x is positive or greater than 0. Within the while loop, we decrement the value of x by 1. Once the value 1 is printed, the value of x becomes 0 and the program exits the while loop.

Continue Statement

We can use a continue statement, just like we used it in the for loop to skip an iteration. In the example below, the value of the variable i is initially set to 0. As long as the value of i is greater than 6 the while block is executed. Within the while loop, we will skip executing the print(i) command when the value of i is 3.

```
i = 0
while i < 6:
    i += 1
    if i == 3:
        continue
    print(i)
```

```
1
2
4
5
6
```

Else Statement

We can use the else statement to gracefully exit the while loop. In the example below, we have initialized the variable i with the value 1. The while loop will run as long as the value of i is less than 6. When the value of 'i' becomes 7 the program enters the else block and then prints "i is no longer than 6."

```
i = 1
```

```
while i < 6:
    print(i)
    i += 1
else:
    print("i is no longer less than 6")
```

```
1
2
3
4
5
i is no longer less than 6
```

Assignment

1. Use a for loop to calculate the sum of all numbers from 1 to 10.
2. Write a program to iterate over a list of numbers from 1 to 100 and display numbers divisible by 5.
3. Display numbers from -10 to 1 using a for loop.

NOTES

Chapter 8: Functions

In this chapter, we will learn about Function in Python and its different uses. Functions are used to avoid code duplication, and writing modular and maintainable code.

8.1 Function vs Method

Python is both a procedural and an object-oriented programming language. A method is the equivalent of a Function in the world of object-oriented programming. We will explore how to declare a method in a class in the section on object-oriented programming.

8.2 Defining a Function

In the last section, we have learned about the difference between a function and a method. In this section, we will learn how to define a function with its correct syntax and usage.

A function is composed of the following components:

a. def keyword
b. Name of the Function
c. Arguments
d. Body of the Function
e. Return type of the Function

Creating a function

You can create a function using the def keyword.

```
def my_function():
    print("Hello from a function")
```

In the above code snippet, the function name is prepended with the def keyword, indicating that this is a function. A function is used to implement a business logic that can be used in different parts of your program.

Let us look at another function with arguments passed to the function.

```
def my_function(arg1, arg2):
    print("Function call with args", arg1, arg2)
```

In the above code snippet, arg1 and arg2 are the two arguments passed to the function. Arguments are defined in parentheses right after the function name. The arguments are separated from each other using commas.

A function needs to be called with the exact number of arguments as defined by the function template.

For example, we would call the function my_function as follows:

```
my_function(1,2)
my_function('Python', 'C++')
```

If you do not know how many arguments your function needs, you can add a "*" before the name of the parameter in the function.

```
def my_function(*kids):
    print("The youngest child is " + kids[2])

my_function("Emil", "Tobias", "Linus")
```

In the above code snippet, the function my_function would display:

```
The youngest child is Linus
```

Linus is the 3rd element that is passed as an argument to the function. Since the indexing starts at 0, the third element is accessed by the 2nd index.

You can also use the key=value syntax to send arguments to the function.

```
def my_function(child3, child2, child1):
    print("The youngest child is " + child3)

my_function(child1="Emil", child2="Tobias", child3="Linus")
```

In the above code snippet, the parameters are passed based on the key-value and could be passed in any order as long as the key values are consistent with the function arguments. The output of the print statement would be:

```
The youngest child is Linus
```

You can also pass a list as an argument.

```
def my_function(food):
    for x in food:
        print(x)

fruits = ["apple", "banana", "cherry"]
my_function(fruits)
```

In the above code snippet, we are passing the list fruits to the function my_function which goes through the list and prints the individual fruit value. The output is as follows:

```
apple
banana
cherry
```

Lists are passed to the functions by pointer or reference, i.e. when a list is passed to the function and if within the function the list value is change, the changes would also be reflected outside the function.

```
def my_function(food):
    food[0] = "New Apple"


fruits = ["apple", "banana", "cherry"]
my_function(fruits)
print(fruits)
```

The above code snippet would modify the fruits list and change the 1st element in the list. The output of the print statement would be as follows:

```
['New Apple', 'banana', 'cherry']
```

```
def add(number1, number2):
     result = number1 + number2
     return result
```

Figure: 8.2

In Figure 8.2 you can see a simple function to add 2 numbers. We define the function by its name called add and use the keyword def before the function name to declare it is a function. The function takes in two parameters as arguments. We have indicated these parameters as number1 and number2. The next core component is the body of the function. We declare a variable called result, which stores the sum of the two numbers, indicated by number1 and number2. The last step is to return the value of the result by using the keyword return.

8.3 Calling a Function

In the last section, you have learned how to declare a Function in Python. In this section, you will learn how to call a function. We will be using the same add function that we saw in the previous section to understand how we can call a function in Python.

The syntax to call a function is to use the name of the function and using a pair of round brackets, i.e. function_name().

Let us imagine we are interested in finding the sum of two numbers. We can call the function add by passing in the two numbers and calling add() from our program.

```
number1= 10
number2 = 5
print(add(number1, number2))
```

Figure 8.3

In the above code snippet, we have declared two numbers, 10 and 5, and called the function add by passing in the two numbers as arguments. We will then use the in -built print function to display the result of the add function, which is the sum of 10 and 5.

8.4 Returning Results from a Function

In the last section, we have explored how to call a function. In this section, we will explore how to return the result of the function using the built-in keyword return.

The add function that we implemented in the previous section uses the keyword return to send back the sum of the two numbers to the caller of the function.

```
return result
```

Figure 8.4

8.5 Returning Multiple Values from a Function

In Python, we can return multiple values from a function. The syn tax that we need to use to send back multiple values is to separate the different values that we wish to send back by a comma. Let us understand the concept of returning multiple values by implementing a simple function to return the names of some countries.

In the Figure 8.5 we have declared a function called get_countries. The function returns the two countries. In order to return the countries, we use the keyword return and separate the two values by a comma.

```
def get_countries():
    return 'India', 'USA'
```

Figure 8.5

```
print(get_countries())
```

Figure 8.6

In Figure 8.6 we can see how we can call the function get_countries and print its return value. We would get the following result, as displayed in Figure 8.6.1.

```
('India', 'USA')
```

Figure 8.6.1

Assignment

1. Write a function to find a square root of a number. The function takes an argument called n, and your task is to return the square root of n.
2. Write a function to find the cube root of a number.
3. Write a function that concatenates two string values and returns the concatenated result.

NOTES

Chapter 9: Modules and Classes

In this chapter, we will learn how to write modular code by learning about object-oriented programming and classes.

Modules

A module is used to organize the functionality of your program as efficiently as possible. A module consists of a Python file that includes a set of related functions and classes. Imagine you are building an image processing application and would like to structure your code to:

1. read and write an image;
2. Perform image processing algorithm on an image;
3. Transform images.

We can have a module for reading and writing an image, a module for image processing, and another module for transforming images.

Let us look at an example.

Open your file editor and create a file called **read_write.py**

```
def read_image(image):
    print('Function to read an image')

def write_image(image):
    print('Function to write an image')
```

Create another file called filtering.py. This file will consist of all image processing algorithms we can perform on an image.

```
def filter_image(image, filter):
    print('Function to smoothen an image')
```

We will create another file called transforms.py. This file will consist of all transformations like cropping, rotation, etc. that we can perform on an image.

```
def transform(image):
    print('Function to transform an image')
```

We can create a file called test.py and import the different modules as follows:

```
from transforms import transform
from filtering import filter_image
from read_write import read_image
```

If we would like to import all the functions and classes within a module, we can use the "*" symbol.

```
from transforms import  *
from filtering import *
from read_write import *
```

Packages in Modules

A package is used to group files belonging to a specific set of modules in a hierarchical structure. You can create a package by initializing the folder with an __init__.py file.

Let us look at an example:

We will create a package called vision and group the modules transforms, filtering, and read_write within this package.

Create a folder called vision and create a new file called __init__.py.

Now copy transforms.py, filtering.py, and read_write.py in the vision folder.

```
.
├── filtering.py
├── __init__.py
├── read_write.py
└── transforms.py
```

In order to expose the files with your packages, open the __init__.py and insert the following code:

```
from .transforms import transform
from .filtering import filter_image
from .read_write import read_image
```

You can now use the functions in the vision package as follows:

```
import vision
vision.read_image()
vision.filter_image()
vision.transform()
```

Classes

In this section, we will learn about an import object-oriented concept called classes. A class is an abstraction or concept on how a feature should behave. Let us take an example of a simple car. A car is characterized by its wheel, color, engine, etc. and behavior like drive, accelerate, brake, etc.

You can initialize a class using the class keyword. Every class needs a constructor. A constructor is used to initialize the car with some basic properties. A constructor is initialized using the __init__ function. Every function within class has the first argument as self.

```
class Car(object):
    def __init__(self, color, brand):
        self.color = color
```

```
        self.brand = brand

    def drive(self):
        print('Car {} with brand {} is driving'.format(self.color,
self.brand))

    def brake(self):
        print('Car {} with brand {} is stopped'.format(self.color,
self.brand))
```

In the above example, we have created a class called Car. In the constructor of the class, we define the color and brand of the car and initialize it by using the self keyword. Every car will be able to drive and brake. To make the example easier to understand, the function will print a line indicating the functionality it is supposed to perform.

```
from Cars import Car

car1 = Car('red', 'BMW')
car1.drive()
car1.brake()

car2 = Car('green', 'Mercedes')
car2.drive()
car2.brake()
```

We can create an instance of the class as shown in the code snippet above.

```
Car red with brand BMW is driving
Car red with brand BMW is stopped
Car green with brand Mercedes is driving
Car green with brand Mercedes is stopped
```

You can change the color of the car as follows:

```
car1. color = 'blue'
car.drive()
car1.brake()
```

The output is as follows:

```
Car blue with brand BMW is driving
Car blue with brand BMW is stopped
```

Deleting attributes

We can delete an attribute or property of a class using the del keyword. Let us look at an example:

```
del car1.color
```

If we now try to execute the drive and brake functionality of the car we will get an error.

```
car1.drive()
car1.brake()
```

```
AttributeError: 'Car' object has no attribute 'color'
```

But we can still access the properties of car2.

```
car2.drive()
car2.brake()
```

```
Car green with brand Mercedes is driving
Car green with brand Mercedes is stopped
```

Assignment

1. Write a class that implements the following functions:
    a. add() - the addition of two numbers
    b. subtract() - the subtraction of two numbers

c. multiplication() - the multiplication of two numbers
d. division() - the division of two numbers

NOTES

Chapter 10: Opening and Closing Files

In this chapter, we will learn about files and some common operations we can perform on files.

As you become more experienced in Python, you would often have to deal with reading text files and extracting data from those files. Let us have a look at some common operations we can perform on files:

1. Reading from a text file
2. Writing to a text file
3. Extracting data from a text file

1. Reading from a text file

   Imagine you are given a text file and would like to access the contents of the file. Create a text file called example.txt with the following contents:

```
Learning Python is fun
Python is a beautiful language
```

   You can now read the contents of the file as follows:

```
with open('example.ext', 'r') as fp:
    data = fp.read()
```

   The above code snippet reads the contents of the files, stores them in the variable called data, and safely closes the file.

2. Writing to a text file

We can append content to an existing file as follows:

```
content = "Hello! Learning Python is easy!"
with open('example.txt', 'a') as fp:
    fp.write(content)
```

If we again read the contents of the file, we will get the following output:

```
'Learning Python is fun\nPython is a beautiful language\nHello! Learning Python
is easy!'
```

3. Accessing contents from a file

Let us now see how we can access the contents of a file and store them in a list.

```
with open('example.txt', 'r') as fp:
    data = fp.read().splitlines()
```

Let us see the contents of data:

```
print(data)
print(type(data))
```

```
['Learning Python is fun', 'Python is a beautiful language', 'Hello!
Learning Python is easy!']
list
```

NOTES

Chapter 11: Map, Filters, and Reduce

In this chapter, we will learn about functional programming in Python by understanding the concept of maps, filters and reduce.

Let us first understand the concept of lambda functions. A lambda function is defined as follows:

lambda arguments: expression

Let us now look at an example of a lambda function.

Imagine you are given a word, and your task is to find the length of the word in the list. We can do this using a lambda function as follows:

```
func_length = lambda x: len(x)
word = "Python"
print(func_length(word))
```

Map

Imagine you want to implement a function to take the square of each and every element in the list. A simple solution to achieve this is as follows:

```
def square(numbers):
    result = []
    for number in numbers:
        result.append(number**2)
    return result

nums = [2,3,4,5,6]
print(square(nums))
```

The output would be as follows:

```
[4,9,16,25,36]
```

We can achieve the same using lambda functions as follows:

```
def square(numbers):
    return list(map(lambda x: x**2, numbers))
```

The map function takes two arguments, a lambda function and a list of numbers. The function can be a lambda function or a normal function that performs an operation on each and every element in the list of numbers. The output of the map function is then converted to a list using the list keyword.

Filters

Filters are used to filter out elements from a list of numbers that meet a specific boolean condition. In the example below, we will implement a function to extract the even numbers from a list of numbers. The filter function also takes two arguments, the lambda function as the first argument, and a list of numbers as the second argument.

```
def get_even_numbers(nums):
    return list(filter(lambda x: x%2==0, nums))

numbers = [1,2,3,4,5,6,7,8,9,10]
print(get_even_numbers(numbers))
```

The output is as follows:

```
[2, 4, 6, 8, 10]
```

Reduce

Reduce functions are functions used to perform some computations on a list of numbers and returning the processed result. Imagine you are given a list of numbers and want to find the product of all the numbers.

```
def product_numbers(numbers):
    return reduce(lambda x,y: x*y, numbers)

numbers = [1,2,3,4,5]
print(product_numbers(numbers))
```

In this chapter we learned how to implement one-line functions such as map, filter, reduce. These functions can be used to improve the quality of your code and reduce the number of lines in your code.

NOTES

Data Structures and Algorithms

In this section, we will learn about essential data structures and algorithms. Learning data structures and algorithms is one of the most important skills you can learn to become an efficient programmer.

Arrays

An array is one of the most fundamental data structures to store data in your computer's memory. An array stores the list of elements in a contiguous block of memory. One of the advantages of using an array is the fast access time. Once we know the index position of an element in an array, we can access that element in O(1) time complexity or constant time.

Some common operations we can perform on an array are:

1. append()
2. clear()
3. copy()
4. count()
5. extend()
6. index()
7. insert()
8. pop()
9. remove()
10. reverse()
11. sort()

Let us see how we can perform some of these operations in Python:

1. append()

   The append operation is used to add elements at the end of the list or array.

```
numbers = [1,3,5,7,8]
print(numbers)
numbers.append(10)
print(numbers)
```

```
[1, 3, 5, 7, 8]
[1, 3, 5, 7, 8, 10]
```

2. clear()
   The clear() method is used to make the array or list empty.

```
numbers.clear()
print(numbers)
```

```
[]
```

3. copy()

The copy() method is used to make a copy of the array and store it in another variable. In the example below, we have created a copy or a replica of the numbers array and stored it in a variable called numbers_copy. The output of the numbers_copy is the same as numbers.

```
numbers = [1,3,5,7,8]
numbers_copy = numbers.copy()
print(numbers_copy)
```

```
[1,3,5,7,8]
```

4. count()

The count() method is used to find out the frequency of occurrence of a number in an array.

```
numbers = [1,3,3,5,5, 7,8]
unique_numbers = set(numbers)
for num in unique_numbers:
    print(num, numbers.count(num))
```

As shown in the output below, all numbers except the numbers 3 and 5 occur once.

```
1 1
3 2
5 2
7 1
8 1
```

5. extend()

The extend() method is used to add the elements of a subarray to the original array at the end of the array. Let us look at an example.

In the example below, we have a sub-array called sub_num, and we add the elements of the sub-array in the arrays indicated by numbers. The output of the numbers array is then the concatenation of the two arrays.

```
numbers = [1, 3, 3, 5, 5, 7, 8]
sub_num = [4,5,12]
numbers.extend(sub_num)
print(numbers)
```

```
[1, 3, 3, 5, 5, 7, 8, 4, 5, 12]
```

6. index()

The index method is used to return the location of the first occurrence of an element in the array. In the example below, we find the first occurrence of the numbers 4 and 6.

```
numbers = [4,5,6,7]
print(numbers.index(4))
print(numbers.index(6))
```

Since the array indexing starts from 0, the first occurrence of 4 is the first element in the array which is indicated by the 0th index in the output and the number 6 is located at the 2nd index or the 3rd position in the array.

```
0
2
```

7. insert()

The insert method is used to add a number at a particular index in the array. In the example below, we add the number at the 1st index. The output after the insertion is shown below, the new number 8 is inserted at the 1st index and the remaining numbers in the original array are shifted to the right by 1.

```
numbers = [5,6,7]
numbers.insert(1, 8)
print(numbers)
```

```
[1,8,6,7]
```

8. pop()

The pop method is used to remove the last element in the array. In the example below, after we call the pop method, the array size is reduced by 1 and the last element is removed from the array.

```
numbers = [5,8,6,7]
numbers.pop()
print(numbers)
```

```
[5,8,6]
```

9. remove()

Just like the insert method, the remove method is used to remove the first occurrence of the given number from the array. In the example below, the number 5 is removed from the array and the output of the array is then [8,6].

```
numbers = [5,8,6]
numbers.remove(5)
print(numbers)
```

```
[8,6]
```

10. reverse()

The reverse method is used to reverse the elements of the array, i.e. the numbers are stored in the opposite direction.

```
numbers = [12,13,14,6,7]
numbers.reverse()
print(numbers)
```

```
[7, 6, 14, 13, 12]
```

11. sort()

The sort method is used to sort the numbers in ascending order.

```
numbers = [33,86,7,12,1]
numbers.sort()
print(numbers)
```

```
[1, 7, 12, 33, 86]
```

Hash Tables

Hash Tables are used to search, insert or delete an element in O(1) time complexity or constant time at the cost of some additional space. In Python, the hash table is implemented using dictionaries. Let us look at some operations we can perform on a hash table.

Let us look at an example. In the example below, we have implemented a function to count the frequency of an element in an array using a hash -map. Using a hash-map, we can find the frequency of any number in an array using constant time complexity.

```
numbers = [1,3,3,5,7,7]
hash_map = {}
for num in numbers:
    if num not in hash_map:
        hash_map[num] = 1
    else:
        hash_map[num] += 1
for key, value in hash_map.items():
    print(key, value)
```

```
1 1
3 2
5 1
7 2
```

Stacks and Queues

Stacks and queues can be built using arrays and linked lists.

A stack is a data structure that works in the principle of LIFO or last-in-first-out or FILO i.e. first-in last-out.

```
numbers = []
numbers.append(12)
numbers.append(13)
numbers.append(14)
top_element = numbers[-1]
print(top_element)
numbers.pop()
top_element = numbers[-1]
print(top_element)
```

```
14
13
```

Queue

A queue is used to insert elements in the FIFO format or first-in first-out format. We can create a queue using a list or the deque library. In the example below we first insert the number 2, then 3, then 5 and in the number 7. We can get the number that is at the beginning of the queue using the 0th index, and we can remove the first number that was inserted using the popleft method. On removing the number 2 the number 3 is at the start of the queue.

```
from collections import deque

queue = deque([2,3,5,7])
print(queue[0])
queue.popleft()
```

```
print(queue[0])
```

```
2
3
```

Binary Search

In this section, we will look at an efficient algorithm to search for a number in an array.

Binary Search is an efficient algorithm to search for a number in 0(logn) time complexity. The algorithm works as follows:

1. Find the middle index of the list.
2. If the number is the middle element of the array, return the middle index.
3. If the number in the middle of the array is greater than the query number, look for the number in the left-half of the array, else look for the number in the right-half of the array.
4. Go to step 1.

```
def binarySearch(numbers, l, h, x):
    if h>=l:
        mid = l + (h-l)//2
        if numbers[mid] == x:
            return mid
        elif numbers[mid] > x:
            return binarySearch(numbers, l, mid-1, x)
        else:
            return binarySearch(numbers, mid+1, h, x)
    else:
        return -1


numbers = [1,8,6,8,3]
print(binarySearch(numbers, 0, len(numbers)-1, 6))
```

Assignment

1. Write a function to merge two sorted arrays.
2. Write a function to find the second maximum element in an array.
3. Given an unsorted array, write a function to sort the array.

NOTES

Common Interview Questions

1. Given a list of numbers from 1 to 100 inclusive, find the missing number in the list

Let us see two approaches to solve this problem:

We know that the sum of n numbers is given by the following formula

$$= \frac{(\ +1)}{2}$$

Now if a number is missing from a list, the result would be the subtraction of the sum of the numbers in the list and the total sum of n numbers.

```
def get_missing_number(l):
    n = len(l) + 1
    sum_list = sum(l)
    total_sum = n*(n+1)/2
    return total_sum - sum_list
```

Let us now generate a list of numbers and call the function get_missing_number.

```
l = list(range(1, 101))
l.remove(55)
print(get_missing_number(l))
```

The result would be 55.

Approach 2

A problem with the first approach is that if n becomes too big, it could lead to integer overflow problems. To solve this problem, we can take the help of the XOR operator.

We know that x XOR x is always 0, so we can first take the XOR of all numbers in the range from 1 to n and another XOR of all the numbers in the list. Finally, we can do an XOR of the result of the previous two operations. All the numbers will be canceled out except the missing number.

```
def get_missing_number_2(l):
    first = 0
    second = 0
    for i in range(1,101):
        first ^= i
    for i in l:
        second ^= i
    return first ^ second
```

2. Find duplicate numbers given a list of numbers

   The naive approach would be to use two *for loops* and compare each number with all the other numbers. The time complexity, however, would be quadratic in nature. Let us look at an efficient approach to solve this problem.

   We can take a hash map or dictionary to store the numbers as we go through the list. As soon as we see a duplicate, we increase the count of that number by 1. We then go through the dictionary and add all keys with a count > 1 since these numbers are duplicates.

```
def find_duplicate(l):
    duplicates = {}
    result = []
    for num in l:
        if num not in duplicates:
            duplicates[num] = 1
        else:
            duplicates[num] += 1
```

```
    for key, value in duplicates.items():
        if value > 1:
            result.append(key)
    return result


l = [2, 2, 2, 3, 4, 3, 6, 4, 3]
print(find_duplicate(l))
```

3. Find the max and min of an unsorted list

   Imagine you are given a list of numbers, and you would like to find the minimum and maximum number in the list. How can we find the min and max without using any python libraries or functions?

   We can keep two variables max_seen and min_seen and assign the first value of the list to both of them. We can then loop through the list starting from the 2nd number in the list and compare each number with the min and max and keep updating both of them. If the number in the list is greater than the max_seen, the max_seen would be updated and if the number in the list is less than the min_seen, the min_seen is updated.

```
def find_min_max(l):
    max_seen = l[0]
    min_seen = l[0]
    for i in range(1, len(l)):
        if l[i] > max_seen:
            max_seen = l[i]
        if l[i] < min_seen:
            min_seen = l[i]
    return min_seen, max_seen

l = [4, 3, 6, 3, 4, 888, 1, -11, 22, 3]
min_number, max_number = find_min_max(l)
```

4. Given a list and a target number, find two numbers in the list whose sum is equal to the target number.

```
def two_sum(l, x):
    start = 0
    end = len(l)-1
    l = sorted(l)
    result = []
    while start < end:
        if l[start] + l[end] == x:
            pair = (l[start], l[end])
            return pair
        elif l[start] + l[end] < x:
            start += 1
        else:
            end -= 1

l = [4, 3, 6, 3, 4, 888, 1, -11, 22,
3] print(two_sum(l, 9))
```

5. Given an array num of n integers where n > 1, return an array output such that output[i] is equal to the product of all the elements of nums except nums[i].

Imagine you are given a list of numbers, and you would like to find the product at an index i such that the product at the index i is equal to the product of all the elements to the left of the index i and the product of all elements to the right of the index.

We can first create a result array and fill it with 0. We define a variable L which keeps track of the product to the left of a particular index. We then define another variable called R which keeps track of the running product from the right and keep updating this value as we loop through the list in reversed order. Let us look at the code below.

```
def productExceptSelf(nums):
    result = [0 for _ in range(len(nums))]
    L = 1
    result[0] = 1
    for i in range(1, len(nums)):
```

```
        result[i] = result[i-1] * nums[i-
    1] R = 1
    for i in reversed(range(len(nums))):
        result[i] = result[i] * R
        R *= nums[i]
    return result

L = [4,5,1,8,2]
print(productExceptSelf(L))
```

6. Given a string, find out if the string is Palindrome or not

A palindrome string is a string which when read from in reverse direction is the same as read from the forward direction. For example, the string ‘radar’ read in both the directions is the same.

We can use a two-pointer approach to solve this problem. We define a variable call i which initially points to the start of the string and another variable called j which points to the last character in the string. We then run a while loop and as long as i < j we check if the character pointed to by the variable i is equal to the string character referenced by the variable j. If it is not equivalent, we return False. If the loop exits successfully, we know that the string is a valid palindrome.

```
def isPalindrome(s):
    i = 0
    j = len(s) - 1
    while i < j:
        if s[i] != s[j]:
            return False
        else:
            i+=1
            j-=1
    return True

test_string = 'radar'
print(isPalindrome(test_string))
```

```
test_string = 'car'
print(isPalindrome(test_string))
```

The output for the string ‘radar’ would be True, whereas the output for the string ‘car’ would be False.

7. Reverse a list in Python

This is a common interview question where you are required to reverse a list in Python without using the reverse function provided by Python. Let us look at the logic of reversing the elements of a list in Python.

We initialize two variables i and j, where i points to the first element of the list and j to the last element of the list. We then run a while loop as long as i is less than j, we swap the elements of the list and increment the i counter by 1 and decrement the j counter by 1. As soon as the program exits the while loop, we return the list, which is a reversed version of the original list.

```
def reverse_list(l):
    i = 0
    j = len(l)-1
    while i < j:
        l[i], l[j] = l[j], l[i]
        i+=1
        j-=1
    return l


l = [1,3,5,9,0]
print(reverse_list(l))
```

The output of the above program is as follows:

```
[0, 9, 5, 3, 1]
```

NOTES

Multiple Choice Questions

1. Which of the following is invalid?

    a. 3name
    b. name
    c. my_name
    d. _name

2. Which of the following is not a keyword?

    a. assert
    b. eval
    c. pass
    d. nonlocal

3. What is the output of the following statement?

```
name = 'Python'
print(name.lower())
```

    a. PYTHON
    b. Python
    c. python
    d. None of the above

4. What is the output of the following statement?

```
a = 4.2
b = 2
print(a//b)
```

a. 2.1
b. 2.0
c. 2
d. None of the above

5. What is the output of the following statement?

```
a = 4
b = 2
c = a/b
print(c)
```

a. 2
b. 2.0
c. None of the above

6. What is the output of the following statement?

```
a = 12
b = 56
c = a+b
del a
print(a)
```

a. 68
b. 12
c. 56
d. None of the above

7. Given a string a = 'Python' what is the output of a? Replace ('y', '++')?

a. 'P++thon'
b. 'Python'
c. None of the above

8. What is the output of the following program?

```python
a = '12'
b = 34
c = a+b
print(c)
```

a. ‘46’
b. 46
c. TypeError
d. None of the above

9. What is the output of the following statement?

```python
a = True
b = False
if a&b:
    print(1)
else:
    print(2)
```

a. 1
b. 2
c. True
d. None of the above

10. Given a list a = [‘Python’, ‘C++’, ‘Java’, ‘Scala’] write the output of the following

statement `print(a[0:2])?`

a. [‘Python’, ‘C++’, ‘Java’, ‘Scala’]
b. [‘Python’, ‘C++’, ‘Java’]
c. [‘Python’, ‘C++’]
d. None of the above

11. Given a list a = [‘Python’, ‘C++’, ‘Java’, ‘Scala’] write the output of the following statement?

```
print(a[-2])
```

a. 'Java'
b. 'Scala'
c. 'C++'
d. None of the above

12. Write the output of the following program:

```
a = ['Python', 'C++']
for word in a:
    word.upper()
print(a)
```

a. ['PYTHON', C++]
b. ['Python', 'C++']
c. ['PYTHON', 'C++']
d. None of the above

13. What is the output of the following program?

```
my_dict = {'name' : 'Mark', 'age': 32, 'location': 'Los Angeles'}
for key, value in my_dict.items():
    print(key, value)
```

a. name Mark
   age 32
   location Los Angeles

b. name MARK
   age 32
   location LOS ANGELES
c. None of the above

Answers

1. 3name is invalid, since a variable name can't start with a number.
2. nonlocal is not a keyword in Python.
3. python is the output when we execute the method lower on the string "Python".
4. 2.0
5. 2.0
6. None of the above.
7. 'P++thon'
8. TypeError.
9. 2
10. ['Python', 'C++']
11. 'Java'
12. ['Python', 'C++']
13. name Mark
    age 32
    location Los Angeles

NOTES

Applications

In this section, we will look at some common applications you can build using Python and its huge ecosystem of libraries.

1. Automation

Many startups around the working on self-driving and automation technologies. Most of the current state-of-the-art computer vision applications are built in Python. You can use a library like OpenCV, TensorFlow, NumPy etc. to develop computer vision and image processing applications.

2. Text Processing

The last decade saw a surge in the number of natural language processing applications. Natural language processing applications are used to develop language translation tools, grammar check tools, sentiment analysis tools. The core of all these algorithms are developed using Python. The demand for people who can develop such production - grade applications will only increase in the coming few years. By completing this book, you have already taken the first step in becoming one of those people who can develop such applications.

3. Web development

With the support of popular frameworks like Fast API, Django and Flask, you can develop robust, secure and reliable backend applications in Python. Some of the most popular websites run using the Django framework. By learning Python, you can advance your journey by learning about web-site development and developing Rest API's in Python

4. Machine Learning and Data Science

Python has a huge support of machine learning libraries and statistical libraries like NumPy, Pandas, Sklearn, etc. You can use these libraries to build machine learning.

applications like recommendation systems, anomaly detection algorithms etc. If you are interested in advancing your journey, you can start learning about Machine Learning.

5. Graphical User Interfaces

Python can also be used to develop graphical user interfaces with popular libraries like PyQt and Dash. You can learn one of these frameworks to start building visualization tools. All of these popular tools have support for Python and if data visualization is something you would like to pursue you could explore this option too.

Popular Python Libraries

In this section, we will discuss some popular Python libraries.

1. NumPy

NumPy is a popular Python library for matrix algebra and vector calculus. If you would like to become a data scientist, having a good grasp of NumPy will help you solve complex problems.

2. Matplotlib

Python is a great programming language because of all the visualization libraries it supports. Matplotlib is one popular library that can help you visualize bar plots, charts, graphs, etc.

3. Scikit-Learn

If you ever decide to become a machine learning engineer, you should have a look at Scikit-learn. Scikit-learn implements some of the most powerful and common machine learning algorithms like linear regression, support vector machines, K-Means clustering, K-Nearest neighbors, decision trees, etc.

4. OpenCV

OpenCV is a popular library for image processing and computer vision. You can find a lot of algorithms for basic image manipulation tasks.

5. Spacy

If you are interested in text processing or implementing some advanced natural language processing algorithms, then Spacy is a popular library with an active developer community.

6. Django

If you would like to become a web-developer, then learning a popular framework like Django can make your life very easy. Django a popular framework based on the MVC or model-view-controller pattern that is actively developed. You can build API's and develop backend applications using Django.

NOTES

Test Your Skills

1. What is the output of the following operation?

```
a = 24/12
print(a)
```

A. The output of the above operation would be a floating point number. The output would be 2.0

2. Is this a valid variable name?

```
_1name = 'Python'
```

A. A variable can start with an underscore symbol, so this is indeed a valid variable name.

3. What is the output of the following operation?

```
x =25*2 +(30-1)/2
print(x)
```

A. The output of the above operation would be 64.5

4. What is the output of concatenating the two strings?

```
a = 'Python'
b = 'is an easy language'
print(a+b)
```

A. The output of the above string concatenation would be 'Python is an easy language'. There is no space after Python, so there will not be any empty space between the two strings.

5. Will the output be True or False?

```
a = 3==3
print(a)
```

A. The above boolean operation would be True, since 3 is indeed equal to 3.

6. Will the output be True or False?

```
countries = ['USA', 'Germany',
'Mexico'] result = 'mexico' in
countries print(result)
```

A. The above output would be False since strings are case-sensitive so ‘mexico is not equal to ‘Mexico’.

7. Convert the string to lowercase.

```
name = 'DATABASE'
```

A. You can convert the string to lowercase using name.lower() function. The output then would be database.

8. Convert the string to uppercase.

```
name = 'operating systems'
```

A. You can convert the string to uppercase using the name.upper() function. The output then would be OPERATING SYSTEMS.

9. Print the length of the string.

```
sentence = 'Learning Python is easy'
#print the length of the string
```

```
length_of_sentence = ?
print(length_of_sentence)
```

A. The length of the sentence would be 23 since while counting the length of the string the empty spaces are also counted.

10. What is the 3rd element of the list. Can you print it?

```
lst = ['Apples', 'Oranges', 'Melon', 'Grapes']
# print the 3rd element of the list
```

A. The 3rd element inf the list is 'Melon' and can be accessed by lst[2] since the indexing in Python starts from 0.

11. What is the output of the following operation?

```
number = 25//11
print(number)
```

The // operator rounds of the result to the nearest whole number. The output of 25//11 would be 2.

12. Write a function to generate a list of n numbers, where n is the parameter passed to the function.

```
def generate_list_numbers(n):
    numbers = [i for i in range(n)]
    return numbers
```

13. Write a function to check if a number is divisible by 2 and 3.

```
def divisible_by_2_and_3(num):
    if num%2==0 and num%3==0:
        return True
```

```
    else:
        return False
```

14. Write a function to check if a number is prime or not.

```
def isPrime(n):
    if n == 1:
        return True
    for i in range(2, int(n/2)+1):
        if n%i==0:
            print('Number {} is not prime'.format(n))
            return False
    print('Number {} is a prime number'.format(n))
    return True
```

15. Write a program to convert the integer 8 to its binary form.

A. You can use the bin function to convert an integer number to its binary representation.

```
binary_repr = bin(8)
print(binary_repr)
```

We get the following output:

```
'0b1000'
```

16. What is the output of the following operation?

```
a = 3 & 8
print(a)
```

A. 3 in its binary form is 0011 and 8 in its binary form is 0100. The and of 0 and 0 is 0, 0 and 1 is 0, 1 and 0 is 0 and 1 and 1 is 1, so the output of 3 & 8 would be 0.

17. Write a program to multiple 3 with 4 using bit-wise left operator.

```
result = 3 << 2
```

18. Write a program to divide 40 by 4 using bit-wise right operator.

```
result = 40 >> 2
```

19. What is __init__ while defining a class in Python?

A. __init__ is used to define the constructor of a class. The constructor is a class that is used to initialize the member variables of the class.

20. What is the difference between lists and tuples?

A. The main difference between a list and a tuple is that the tuple is immutable, whereas a list is mutable.

21. What are local variables and global variables in Python?

A. A local variable is valid within the scope of a function and does not exist outside the scope of the function, whereas a global variable is also valid outside the scope of a local function.

22. How can you convert a string to int?

A. You can convert a string to int by casting the string to int.

Imagine there is number num = '10', you can cast it to an int as

follows num_int = int(num)

23. Can you convert the string to int?

```
num = '45'
# convert string to integer
```

```
num_integer = # write your code here
print(num_integer)
print(type(num_integer))
```

```
num = '45'
num_integer = int(num)
print(num_integer)
print(type(num_integer))
```

The output is as follows:

```
45
<class 'int'>
```

24. Is indentation required in Python?

A. Yes, indentation is required in Python or else you will get a syntax

error. 25. What is self in Python?

A. In object-oriented programming, the self keyword represents the instance of a class, and it is used to access the member variables and functions of the class.

26. Can you write a function to randomly generate a list of numbers between 1 and n?

```
import random

def generate_random_numbers(n, k):
    numbers = [random.randint(1, n+1) for _ in
    range(k)] return numbers
print(generate_random_numbers(100, 10))
```

27. What is a dictionary in Python?

A. A dictionary in Python is used to construct a hash-map in Python. It is represented with two curly braces {}.

28. Write a function to print the product of the following two matrices.

A = [[1,2], [3,4]]
B = [[1,2,3,4,5], [5,6,7,8,9]]

```
def matrix_mul(A, B):
    # write your code
    number_of_rows_A = len(A)
    number_of_rows_B = len(B)

    current_row_A = 0
    current_column_A = 0
    current_row_B = 0
    current_column_B = 0
    if len(A[0]) != len(B):
        return 'Not possible'

    C=[]
    for i in range(0, number_of_rows_A):
        sublist = []
        for j in range(0, len(B[0])):
            sublist.append(0)
        C.append(sublist)

    while current_row_A < number_of_rows_A:
        number_of_columns_A = len(A[current_row_A])
        while current_column_B < len(B[0]):
                for row_B in range(0, number_of_rows_B):
                    C[current_row_A][current_column_B] +=
   A[current_row_A][row_B] * B[row_B][current_column_B]
            current_column_B += 1
        current_row_A += 1
        current_column_B = 0
    return(C)
```

```
A   = [[1,2],[3,4]]
B   = [[1,2,3,4,5] ,[5,6,7,8,9]]
matrix_mul(A, B)
```

The output is as follows:

```
[[11, 14, 17, 20, 23], [23, 30, 37, 44, 51]]
```

29. Given a string, write a function to replace the digits in the string with the "#" character. Return the update string value.

```
def replace_digits(String):
    result_string = ''
    for char in String:
        if char.isdigit():
            result_string += '#'
    return result_string

String = '#2a$#b%c%561#'
print(replace_digits(String))
```

30. Can you write a function to sort the numbers in an unsorted

list? You can use the sort method to sort a list.

```
nums = [1,81,46,0,3,-8]
nums.sort()
```

The output is as follows:

```
[-8, 0, 1, 3, 46, 81]
```

A FREE GIFT TO OUR READERS

7 surprising beginner mistakes you should avoid as a beginner programmer downloadable guideline. This will set you on the right path to learning how to program.

santosbooks.com

Conclusion

Congratulations! You have finally reached the end of this book. You learned a lot about the basics of programming, writing statements, understanding variables, functions, and additional data structures like Tuples, Lists, and Dictionaries.

This is, however, just the beginning. There is still a lot to explore and with the knowledge, you have gained through this book you are well set up to transition into a successful Python developer. You can improve your Python skills by solving coding problems on platforms like leetcode or Project Euler. If you would like to transition into the field of data science, you can get started by exploring libraries like NumPy, Matplotlib, and learn.

Appendix

Guess the number!

In this section, we will implement a simple guess the number application. The application will generate a random number, and the user would have to guess the number that the application generated. Let us look at how we can implement such an application.

We will first import the random library to generate random numbers.

```
import random
```

We can generate random numbers using the randint function.

```
print(random.randint(1,100))
```

The randint function takes two arguments a and b, i.e. the interval in which the number should be generated. In the above example, we will generate a number between 1 and 100.

We can ask for an input number from the user using the input function. We will then convert this number into int to compare the input number with the random number.

```
number = int(input())
```

Our logic would be to keep comparing the number with the random number for a set number of attempts. If the user manages to guess the correct number, we will print "You guessed the correct number" and end the game. If the number guessed by the user was less than the random number, we will ask the user to guess a higher larger number, whereas if the number input by the user was greater than the random number, we will ask the user to choose a lower number. We can put this entire logic in a while loop. We will also add a feature to keep running this loop for a set number of attempts.

Let us first define a variable called current_attempt and assign it a value of 0.

```
current_attempt = 0
max_attempt = 10
```

Let us now look at the logic of implementing the while loop.

```
x = random.randint(1,100)
while current_attemp <= max_attempt:
    number = int(input())
    if number == x:
        print('You guessed the correct number')
    elif number < x:
       print('The number was small! Guess again!')
    elif number > x:
       print('The number was large! Guess again!')
    current_attempt += 1
```

We can put the entire functionality in a function called guess number. You can find the entire code below:

```
import random

def guess_number(x, attempts=10):
    current_attempt = 0
    while current_attempt <= attempts:
        number = int(input())
        if number == x:
            print('You guessed the correct number')
            return
        elif number < x:
            print('The number was small! Guess again!')
        elif number > x:
            print('The number was big!Guess again!')
        current_attempt += 1
    print('All attempts exhausted!')
x = random.randint(1,100)
guess_number(x)
```

You can see the output below:

```
100
The number was big!Guess again!
12
The number was small! Guess again!
50
The number was small! Guess again!
60
The number was small! Guess again!
70
The number was small! Guess again!
80
The number was big!Guess again!
75
The number was big!Guess again!
73
The number was small! Guess again!
74
You guessed the correct number
```

Leetword representation of a sentence

In this section, we will look at a program to find out the leetword representation of a sentence. A leetword replaces the character a with 4, b with 8, e with 3, l with 1, o with 0, s with 5 and t with the number 7. We need to write a program that converts a string to its leetword representation.

We will first create a hash map as follows:

```
mapping = {'a' : 4, 'b' : 8, 'e' : 3, 'l':1,
           'o': 0, 's': 5, 't' : 7
           }
```

Now we can iterate over the words in the string and iterate over each character in the word to find out if the char exists in the hash map or not. If it does, we will replace that character with its leetword representation, else we will keep the same character in the resulting string.

You can find the entire code snippet below:

```
def leetword(s):
 mapping = {'a' : 4, 'b' : 8, 'e' : 3, 'l':1,
      'o': 0, 's': 5, 't' : 7
            }
   result = ""
  for word in s.split(" "):
        for char in word:
            if char in mapping:
                result += str(mapping[char])
            else:
                result += char
        result += " "
    return result

res = leetword("I like to eat eggs and spam")
print(res)
```

The output is as follows:

```
'I 1ik3 70 347 3gg5 4nd 5p4m '
```

Printed in Great Britain
by Amazon

77599906R00084